Cavendish Prac

Debt Recovery

Third Edition

Stephen Paul Allinson, LLB (Hons), FABRP, MICM, Licensed Insolvency Practitioner

Series Editor
CM Brand, Solicitor

Cavendish
Publishing
Limited

London • Sydney

Third edition first published in Great Britain 2001 by Cavendish
Publishing Limited, The Glass House, Wharton Street, London
WC1X 9PX, United Kingdom
Telephone: +44 (0)20 7278 8000   Facsimile: +44 (0)20 7278 8080
Email: info@cavendishpublishing.com
Website: www.cavendishpublishing.com

British Library Cataloguing in Publication Data. A catalogue
record for this book is available from the British Library.

ISBN 1 85941 449 4

Printed and bound in Great Britain

To my father: in the hope that I can be to my children as he was to me.

Preface

Since the second edition of this book was published, much of civil litigation has undergone fundamental change, most notably with the new procedural system that is now in place for the majority of cases. This edition therefore focuses on how debt recovery litigation should be conducted in the light of the Civil Procedure Rules 1998 and all the developments that have flowed from those changes. At the same time, however, the process of reform is not complete in the field of debt recovery. The Government has indicated that it wishes to carry out a reform of the enforcement process, although as yet that is very much at the consultation stage. Thus, inevitably, the way lawyers utilise debt recovery procedures will develop further over the coming years.

Throughout this book there are regular references to the importance of ensuring that the most up to date information is utilised, particularly with regard to amendments to the Civil Procedure Rules; court fees, costs and court forms both in the High Court and county court. That advice is never more relevant than at this time of possible further development in the way debt recovery proceedings are undertaken.

Stephen Allinson
March 2001

Acknowledgments

There are several people whom I must thank for enabling the third edition of this book to come to fruition. A number of my colleagues have offered practical advice and guidance (and where necessary pointed out errors). In this regard I trust Claire Sharp has found her assistance a valuable part of her legal training. In particular, however, I would like to thank Jane Dunlop, head of Clarke Willmott & Clarke's Business Recovery Unit for her detailed reading of the manuscript and for ensuring that this is a practical as well as theoretical analysis of the law. My secretary, Caroline Lismer, typed the last edition and has once again undertaken the whole of the typing and word processing work that is crucial to any project and I thank her very much.

My wife Glenys not only ensured that I knuckled down to complete the book but also undertook the detailed proof reading of each chapter and ensured corrections were identified. Any mistakes that remain are my own. To Glenys, and my children, Emma and Susannah, who (unlike when the first two editions were written) now understand what is involved in writing a book, I offer my total thanks for making the long hours worthwhile.

The law, as I understand it, is correct as at March 2001.

Stephen Allinson
March 2001

Contents

1 Basic Information

1.1 Introduction

The recovery of money for clients has always been an important aspect of a solicitor's work. The pace of business life will continue to increase, and so clients, both personal and corporate, will require their debts to be collected, quickly and efficiently to ensure their business does not suffer. In a recessionary time, the collection of debts by a solicitor for a client could be the difference between survival and failure for that client. In addition, the solicitor's role in this field must include detailed attention to the avoidance of bad debts for clients and the setting up of efficient systems of credit control.

This book aims to provide a simple and concise procedural and practical guide to debt recovery in both the High Court and county court, with reference to the various remedies available. Emphasis is on the enforcement of a judgment rather than the procedural steps leading up to that judgment. Reference should be made (where appropriate) to other relevant Cavendish Practice Notes in the series: *County Court Procedure*; *Contentious Costs*; and *Insolvency Law*.

1.2 Sources

A working knowledge of the legal sources of reference is essential for efficient debt recovery. In this regard, the whole area of debt recovery (as with civil litigation generally) has been completely revolutionised.

1.2.1 Background to the changes

The Government's White Paper *Modernising Justice* was presented to Parliament in December 1998 and consisted of a complete review of the justice system. Prior to this document, Lord Woolf had produced

his final *Access to Justice* report in July 1996 and, although the Government's review covered all aspects of the legal system, in terms of the civil justice system, Lord Woolf's proposals resulted in the appearance of the Civil Procedure Rules 1998 SI 1998/3132. It is these Rules (as subsequently amended and updated) which now form the basis of debt recovery actions commenced through the legal system. They came into force on 26 April 1999 but since that time have been subject to numerous amendments and updates, together with related Practice Directions and it is essential that all those practising in this area keep themselves fully up to date with these rules. At the time of writing, the rules had seen some 21 amendments by way of updates. One way of ensuring the most up to date version of the rules is available is to utilise the resources that are now available on the world wide web for lawyers. Many legal sites will have links to the Civil Procedure Rules (referred to subsequently in this book as CPR) but a good starting point is the Lord Chancellor's Department web site whose home page can be found at:
http://www.open.gov.uk/lcd/index.htm

The CPR is divided into parts. Each part is then divided into rules. If references to rules are given, the correct way to deal with this is not by reference to a part. Thus Rule 1 in Part 1 describes the overriding objective of the CPR and that is described as CPR 1.1. This method of description will be adopted throughout this book.

1.2.2 The Civil Procedure Rules and debt recovery

Debt recovery actions are of course only one type of action that go through the Courts. Subsequent chapters will refer to the particular rules which affect particular aspects of any debt recovery action. There are however some fundamental aspects of these Rules which should be borne in mind by way of an introduction and overview and these are as follows:

1.2.2.1 The overriding objective of the reforms is to deal with cases justly, proportionately, expeditiously and fairly (CPR Part 1).

1.2.2.2 As part of this overall objective, the courts will become much more involved in the verification process and will to a large extent drive it through the new concept of case management. In many cases, the court will set the timetable, rather than the parties to the action, and will seek to drive the parties to appropriate resolutions. Part of the case management will be the allocation of all actions to the particular 'track' at an early stage and depending on which track is allocated, the appropriate process will follow the Rules of that track.

1.2.2.3 The emphasis of these Rules and of the reforms generally is to seek to resolve issues without final court hearings. They embrace the concepts of mediation and alternative dispute resolution which increasingly form part of our civil justice system.

1.2.2.4 Under the new Rules, the courts will have greater power and flexibility with regard to awarding costs. The theory behind these powers is that making parties realise the costs of any litigation action as it proceeds to a greater degree than in the past should concentrate the minds of the parties into resolving the issues.

1.2.2.5 The Civil Procedure Rules are helpfully categorised into parts (replacing the previous references to Orders which were a standard feature of the old system).

For the lawyer involved in debt recovery, the following Parts will often be relevant:

Part 1   Overriding objective.

Part 3   The courts' case management powers.

Part 6   Service of documents.

Part 7   How to start proceedings – the claim form.

Part 12   Default judgment.

Part 22   Statements of truth.

Part 24   Summary judgment.

Part 27   The small claims track.

Part 28   The fast track.

Part 29   The multi track.

Part 36   Offers to settle and payments into court.

Parts 43–48 Costs.

Part 51   Transitional arrangements (insofar as any action crosses the boundaries between the previous rules and the present ones).

1.2.3 Rules of the Supreme Court and County Court Rules

Previous editions of this text have made numerous references to the Rules of the Supreme Court 1965 SI 1965/1776 and the County Court Rules 1981 SI 1981/1687 and the appropriate books that support those Rules (the White Book and the Green Book). These Rules are still to some extent relevant. Pursuant to CPR Part 50, the Rules that remain are set out as schedules to the new Rules; the Rules of the Supreme Court are set out at Sched 1 and the County Court Rules as at Sched 2. For the lawyer undertaking debt recovery, it is important to realise that the enforcement provisions still remain. However, it should be noted that the procedures whereby a judgment is enforced in either the county court or High Court are currently the subject of discussion and consultation and it is anticipated that further reforms of the enforcement process will follow in the not too distant future. At the present time, however, for the purposes of debt recovery the following are the most important Rules of the Supreme Court which remain relevant and in force subsequent to the onset of the Civil Procedure Rules (see CPR Sched 1):

RSC Order 10   Service of originating process.

RSC Order 30   Receivers.

RSC Order 45   Enforcement of judgments and orders: general.

RSC Order 46   Writs of execution: general.

RSC Order 47   Writs of *fieri facias*.

RSC Order 48   Examination of judgment debtor.

RSC Order 49   Garnishee proceedings.

RSC Order 50   Charging orders.

RSC Order 51   Receivers – equitable execution.

As for the County Court Rules 1981, for the purposes of debt recovery, the following are the most relevant orders which remain either in whole or in part (see CPR Sched 2):

CCR Order 3   Commencement of proceedings.

CCR Order 4   Venue for bringing proceedings.

CCR Order 5   Causes of action and parties.

CCR Order 6   Particulars of claim.

CCR Order 7   Service of document.

CCR Order 16   Transfer of proceedings.

CCR Order 25   Enforcement of judgments and orders: general.

CCR Order 26   Warrants of execution, delivery and possession.

CCR Order 27   Attachments of earnings.

CCR Order 28   Judgment summonses.

CCR Order 30   Garnishee proceedings.

CCR Order 31   Charging orders.

CCR Order 32   Receivers.

CCR Order 39   Administration orders.

1.3 Costs

The varying figures for costs (often called fixed costs) that are awarded in debt actions in both the High and the county courts are reviewed regularly and care should always be taken to ensure that the correct costs are claimed. In general terms, there are fixed costs for the standard steps in a debt recovery action (Chapter 17 sets out the most common costs and fees at the date of publication). It should be remembered that fees have to be paid to the court for most steps that are taken in an action, for example, the issue of proceedings and the taking of the various enforcement steps. The fixed costs that the court awards throughout the action invariably do not equate to the true cost of a solicitor's time. With this in mind, it is vital that an accurate procedure is agreed at the commencement of the solicitor/client relationship for accounting purposes.

1.4 Debt collection terms

Debt recovery and debt collection has developed its own glossary of terms and reference will be made to these throughout the text but the following phrases occur regularly.

1.4.1 Letter before action

This describes the letter that clients and solicitors invariably write putting the debtor on notice that proceedings will be commenced unless payment is received within a time period (or by a date specified in that letter) which by tradition is not less than seven days (a sample letter before action is set out in Chapter 3 at 3.3.1.).

1.4.2 Small claims court

Technically, there is no such thing as a small claims court, but clients often refer to this when considering collecting debts not exceeding £5,000 in the county court. Currently, any proceedings for a sum not exceeding this figure are in the vast majority of cases allocated to the small claims track and dealt with under a more informal procedure (CPR Part 27). The general rule is that no solicitors' costs are recoverable in this procedure except the costs on the issue of the claim, and, therefore, for such claims, a client could find it expensive to utilise a solicitor.

1.4.3 Terms and conditions

Clients will often refer to their 'terms and conditions' and refer to invoices and quotations containing these. The terms and conditions printed thereon will be an attempt to protect themselves in the event of there being problems with the payment of money pursuant to a particular contract. Such terms and conditions may vary in length and complexity considerably. The solicitor should ensure he has a copy of this document or documents before advising clients on debt recovery.

1.4.4 Retention of title

A phrase used to describe a clause that often appears in terms and conditions of trading. This is an attempt by clients to prevent ownership of goods that have been supplied by them passing to the debtor until payment in full has been made. The courts have usually found that the more complicated these clauses are, the less likely they are to be legally binding.

1.4.5 The battle of the forms

This describes colloquially the procedure whereby in most contracts both parties may seek to obtain the contract on their standard terms and conditions. The general view is that the party which fires the last shot (that is, supplies the last set of terms and conditions in the contractual scenario) will ensure his terms and conditions prevail.

1.4.6 Bad debt

A bad debt is a non-recoverable debt. The phrase is often used by accountants who wish solicitors to advise upon whether or not certain debts should be classed as such for the purposes of annual accounts. It also has relevance for VAT relief if a debt is not recovered.

1.4.7 Normal credit period

Many businesses and professions allow a period of time (often one month) in which an account can be settled, and this is called the normal credit period.

1.4.8 The District Judge

This is the person who will deal with all interim stages in a debt recovery action and, pursuant to his jurisdiction he may also deal with final hearings. He is a senior lawyer (more often than not a solicitor).

1.4.9 Court Bailiff

The officer of the court charged by the District Judge to execute warrants of execution for creditors, which is the procedure whereby he seeks to seize goods of the debtor and sell the same to settle the debt.

1.4.10 High Court Sheriff

The officer of the court who carries out similar functions to the county court Bailiff under High Court procedure.

1.4.11 Conduct money

A phrase used to describe the sum of money paid or tendered to a debtor being a reasonable sum for his travelling expenses to attend court. Such money is sometimes a prerequisite to the carrying out of certain enforcement steps (as will be seen in subsequent chapters), for example, on an adjourned hearing of an oral examination or judgment summons.

2 Avoiding Bad Debts

2.1 Knowing your client

The most efficient system of debt recovery is obviously to ensure that debts do not arise. Effective steps should therefore be taken at the outset by clients and their solicitor to prevent debt problems occurring.

2.2 Preventative advice to the client

When acting for a client, a solicitor should always take time to review the credit control system that is utilised by the client and, if necessary, suggest amendments and refinements. Systems can be either manual or computer based; can vary in complexity depending on the nature of the business, but must always be a proactive system rather than a reactive one. The advantage of a solicitor being involved at the outset with a credit control system is that familiarity will be present if that system is then the basis for subsequent legal action.

When undertaking a new contractual relationship, the client should be in a position to assess the risks of contracting and have some background knowledge of the person with whom he wishes to deal. The use of a standard *proforma* by clients requiring personal or company details to be completed has considerable advantages and some of that information can be used later if problems develop and the solicitor is asked to advise.

2.2.1 Bank references

Bank references are often utilised, but their effectiveness is perhaps questionable. The information given is usually limited. It is often more important to analyse what is not stated than what is.

2.2.2 Trade references

A trade reference may be of more use, particularly if the client is himself a trader or has contacts in that field. Care should be taken, however, to check the authenticity of such references if they come from an unknown source.

2.2.3 Credit references

It may be worthwhile to consider using a credit reference agency. There are many companies offering such credit services. For a prescribed fee, such an agency will supply known information on the creditworthiness of a debtor, for example, details of any county court judgments. If dealing with a company, the credit reference agency will often combine this information with a full company search. Care should be taken to ensure that more money is not expended than is necessary in obtaining this information, as credit reference and company search information can often be duplicated.

2.2.4 Register of county court judgments

Remember that it is only county court (surprisingly not High Court) judgments that are registered. Since 1 April 1990, all county court judgments are registered on judgment, with the exception of genuine defended cases where the losing party does not request an instalment order. In addition, pursuant to the Register of County Court Judgments (Amendment) Regulations 1993 SI 1993/710, administration orders are registered as from 31 March 1993. In addition, orders restricting enforcement are also registered.

This Register is kept pursuant to s 73A of the County Court Acts 1984 and is under the control of Registry Trust Ltd, 173–75 Cleveland Street, London W1P 5PE (telephone: (020) 7380 0133).

Upon payment of a fee per named person at a specified address to the above organisation and completion of the form that is supplied by them, the Register will be searched and the amount of judgment, date of judgment and court and claim number of any judgment revealed will be supplied. Such judgment details remain registered for a period of six years.

Copies of the form can be obtained by telephoning the company, and a sample copy is shown in Appendix A.

For full details of the registration procedures from 1 April 1990, reference should be made to the Register of County Court Judgments (Amendment) Regulations 1990 SI 1990/491 and the Register of County Court Judgments (Amendment) Regulations 1991 SI 1991/1815. These Regulations amend the 1985 Register of County Court Judgments Regulations and include details of the cancellation procedure when payment has been made.

At the time of writing, the fees to be paid in respect of searches of the Register are as follows:

- £4.00 per name and address for a request in person, and
- £4.50 per name and address for request by post.

(These fees are obviously subject to change.)

It should be remembered that it is the responsibility of the person against whom the judgment has been registered to apply for a certificate of satisfaction if he requires that to be noted on the register. Furthermore, if a judgment debt is satisfied in full within one month of its date of entry, he is entitled to have the entry in the Register cancelled, but it is his responsibility to make that application. Both certificates of satisfaction and cancellation require application to court where judgment has been obtained and there is a £10.00 fee to be paid.

Alternatively, credit agencies will often provide this service as part of their standard charges (possibly at a more expensive rate, although speed of response could be quicker). It is not possible to undertake telephone searches of the Register of County Court Judgments.

2.2.5 Company searches

When dealing with a company, a search of the Companies Register through reputable company agents is almost a prerequisite of contracting or otherwise dealing. A fee of approximately £25.00 is normally incurred, but this could be money well spent. A lower charge is made for supply of company microfiche which can be obtained direct from Companies House (and a credit account can be opened). Alternatively, a personal visit to Companies House would obtain the same information. It is situated at Crown Way, Cardiff. Further, with the ongoing march of information technology, it is now possible to search the register 'on line' and have direct accounts. The Companies House website can be found at **http://www.companieshouse.gov.uk/index.html**. A telephone search will provide details of the registered office address and confirmation as to whether a liquidator or receiver has been appointed.

A full company search should reveal details of the registered office of the company; the directors, secretary and shareholdings; details of any charges or debentures; and a full copy of the latest filed accounts.

Points to watch out for in company accounts:

- Have they been filed? The Companies Act 1985 provides strict filing requirements for the filing of accounts at Companies House (in general terms, 10 months from the relevant year end). If up to date accounts have not been filed, ascertain the reason for this.
- What do the profit and loss accounts and balance sheet show and are these better figures than the previous years?
- Have there been recent changes of directors? If so, try and ascertain the reason why.
- If bank debentures or charges are revealed, how recently were these taken? Obviously, the larger the debt, the more important this information becomes.
- The company search will reveal, according to the Register, whether or not a company is in receivership or liquidation. It will not, however, reveal whether a winding-up petition has been commenced against that company. Therefore, it is good practice to telephone the Companies Court to discover this information (telephone: (020) 7947 7328) (see 3.1.3).

Remember, however, this information could be somewhat historical and should not be used as a substitute for very up to date information.

2.2.6 Terms and conditions of trading

Although lawyers make much of this subject many clients do not utilise effective terms and conditions of trading. Common pitfalls include:

- a failure to incorporate the terms and conditions at the outset of trading;
- a failure to deal adequately with the other side's terms and conditions ('the battle of the forms');
- a failure to cover all necessary eventualities if the contractual relationship fails.

(a) *Effective incorporation of terms and conditions*: It is not enough simply to reveal terms and conditions of trading at the delivery of goods stage, nor on any invoice that is attached. It may not be sufficient to have the copy of the terms and conditions available at the place where the contract is concluded, unless specific attention is brought to the same. For the avoidance of doubt, the best solution is for a copy of the terms and conditions to be produced to the other side prior to the contract and for a signature to be obtained agreeing that goods will be supplied on those terms and conditions.

(b) *The battle of the forms*: This doctrine means in essence that the party which delivers the last form with terms and conditions will, in the vast majority of cases, ensure that its terms and conditions are the relevant ones for the contract. Ensure therefore that the client's terms and conditions are the final document. If possible, the client should have his terms and conditions endorsed by the other side as being the binding contractual terms.

(c) *Establish a course of dealing*: Even if your client has not delivered on each occasion his terms and conditions, if a customer has been dealt with regularly, then, providing the terms and conditions were brought to his attention at the outset of the trading relationship (or even at a later stage), it may be possible to establish to the court's satisfaction a course of dealing and the incorporation of your client's terms and conditions. This doctrine is, however, fraught with uncertainty and it is much better to ensure that all terms and conditions are set out at the beginning of contract negotiations, and indeed subsequently where relevant. Remember as well that although it perhaps does no harm to include the terms and conditions on a quotation, one interpretation of contractual negotiations could be that a quotation is simply an invitation to treat rather than an offer and is accordingly a pre-contract document, and therefore not binding.

(d) *Effective terms and conditions*: Any work of this nature cannot possibly deal with the myriad of terms and conditions that could be entered into in any contractual relationship. Certain examples, however, of some important terms and conditions are set out below:

- Price and payment clauses – make provision for increase if possible, with a price variation clause.

- Interest – provide for payment of contractual interest in default of payment of an account within a specified period.

- Specified credit terms – for example, 28 days before interest becomes payable.

- Reservation of title clause – this is a most complicated area of law. In essence, it is an attempt by a seller to prevent a buyer owning goods until payment in full has been made and if payment in full is not made, the seller is entitled to recover those goods. This may sound satisfactory in theory, but in practice, there are a number of problems. Consider, for example, if the goods, when they come into the hands of the buyer, become mixed with other goods or become involved in a manufacturing process so that they are not readily identifiable. It is also quite a common situation for a buyer to sell those goods on to a third party (who may or may not know of the reservation of title clause). Thus, there have been a number of attempts to create wide and complicated reservation of title clauses which, in general terms, have not found favour with the courts.

These clauses are most often tested when the company with whom the client is dealing goes into receivership or liquidation and your client effectively does battle with the receiver or liquidator. The following points will almost certainly be relevant:

- The receiver or liquidator will ask for evidence that the goods can be identified.

- The receiver or liquidator will ask for evidence that the relevant clause was incorporated into the contract between the parties.

- The receiver or liquidator will consider very closely the wording of the clause and what has happened to the goods themselves.

- The receiver or liquidator will ask whether or not the clause has been registered under s 395 of the Companies Act 1985. It is now established law that a clause which gives a creditor rights over 'mixed' goods or rights over the proceeds of any resale of those goods will be classified as a charge and, therefore, must be registered pursuant to the Companies Act 1985. A failure to register will render the clause void (regardless of other arguments).

  Accordingly, caution must be undertaken when advising or drafting these clauses. The law in this area is constantly evolving and reference should be made, therefore, to the most recent cases. As a general rule of drafting, the clause should be kept as simple as possible.

- International contracts – with businesses now becoming more international, it is not unusual for dealings to be with companies or individuals in other countries. To that end, ensure that there is an effective choice of law term in the contract which provides that in the event of a dispute, then the relevant law will be that of the country in which the client is based (normally, of course, English law), and that the courts of that country will have jurisdiction.

2.2.7 Personal guarantees from directors

If dealing with a company for the first time or if the history of that company is not promising, consider obtaining a personal guarantee from the directors (or possibly a cross-guarantee from another company, perhaps in the same group).

The desire or otherwise of the directors to give such guarantee may be indicative of the status of the company. The type and form of such guarantee will inevitably vary and if it is too strict, it may have an adverse effect and the customer may not wish to deal on those terms. Alternatively, if drafted in a general way, it may not protect the client in every circumstance which later occurs. At the end of the day, a commercial decision must be taken by the client with his solicitor as to how detailed such a clause should be.

3 Pre-Legal Action Considerations

3.1 Taking instructions

It is generally only when earlier steps have failed that clients turn to solicitors for the collection of outstanding debts. At this stage, it is vital that solicitors act promptly, efficiently and correctly. It is also at this stage that the importance of a client questionnaire is seen. In addition, the better the procedures that have been adopted by the client, the more chance there is of a successful recovery. The background as to the collection of the debt may vary as will the amount involved, but the procedures are similar. At the first appointment, ensure the client brings in all necessary paperwork in connection with the debt, in particular:

- The invoice document upon which the debt is based.
- Any terms and conditions of trading which it is alleged became incorporated in to the contract.
- Any pre-contract correspondence.
- Correspondence between the client and the debtor post-contract.
- Any up to date ledger account showing any monies received.

With this information before you, the obtaining of the initial instructions becomes easier and at the first interview, a checklist for initial instructions can be completed.

3.1.1 Standard *proforma* for use by solicitor

An example of the type of relevant information that a solicitor will require when acting for a client in debt recovery, which should be obtained at the first meeting, is set out below. Although each case will clearly vary considerably, a solicitor should ensure that as many of the following points as possible are obtained at the initial interview.

Section A – Client

- Name.
- Address (or registered office if company); and all trading addresses if a business.
- Particulars of trade or business contact person (credit manager, director, etc).
- Contact telephone number and/or fax number and/or email address(es) and website.

Section B – Details of debtor and debt

- Name of debtor – individual or company.
- Address, registered office, and trading address (if different).
- Trade name.
- Bank account details.
- Partnership – full names of the partners and private addresses.
- Company – full names and addresses of all directors.
- Details of how debt arose (copies of the invoices, etc; dates of any payments made).
- Copies of any correspondence received or sent by client in relation thereto.
- Indication by client of possible dispute which may form a defence/counterclaim.

Section C – Terms and conditions of trading

- Production of terms and conditions of trading by client.
- Details of credit period allowed (seven, 14 or 30 days or end of month following invoice date).
- Is contractual interest claimed by client – if so, at what rate?
- Is there a retention of title clause? If so is it likely to be effective?
- Were any terms and conditions supplied by the debtor? (If so, obtain a copy and ascertain from your client when it was supplied.)
- The battle of the forms – who fired the last shot? When was it fired?

Section D – Miscellaneous

- Have any payments been made – if so, when and how were they credited? If by cheque, obtain the bank details.

- Has any other person guaranteed the debts of the debtor to the client?

- Is any information known concerning the financial security of the defendant? For example, is any property owned upon which security could be taken?

- Has a company search been undertaken or credit check made.

- Are there any known assets of value?

Section E – The continuation of the action

- How often should reports be made to the client – weekly, monthly or otherwise?

- Is the client prepared to proceed to formal insolvency procedure if necessary?

- What costs limit has been placed on action by the client before review?

3.1.2 Further useful information

It may be necessary at this point to undertake some of the searches and inquiries described in 2.2 if these have not been undertaken by the client at an early stage.

Perhaps the best information can be obtained from the client himself. Alternatively, a knowledgeable and well informed enquiry agent may well be able to provide certain information at reasonable cost. Instructions should always be sought from the client as to how far this pre-action process should be taken. If very little is know about the debtor, however, then it may be sensible and result in a saving of money in the long run.

3.1.3 Other searches and register

- Land Charges Registry. A search against the debtor's name at this registry may reveal second or third mortgages (as these have to be registered) and may therefore supply useful information as to whether a charging order should be contemplated in the future. In addition, they may reveal whether there are previous charging orders or alternatively whether there are bankruptcy proceedings pending or a Bankruptcy Order made. The cost is £1.00 per name. The address of the Land Charges Registry is Search Section, Burrington Way, Plymouth PL5. If this search is undertaken, it is important that the debtor's full names are known. An incorrect search will not provide protection. It may be advisable to search not only against the full name of the debtor (including Christian names), but also against the surname and initials as certain registrations may be undertaken in this way.

Telephone inquiries can also be made of the Land Charges Department (telephone: (0845) 308 4545). The Registry is also online, but for both telephone inquiries and on line inquiries, the results are posted rather than delivered in any other manner.

- Land Registry. The Land Registry is of course utilised for all land that has a registered title (and more and more property falls into this category). If there is uncertainty, however, as to whether or not the land is registered, then an official search of the index map can be undertaken to ascertain this and discover the title number. Form 96 (Official Search of Index Map) is utilised for this purpose and is a free facility. It is essential that the fullest possible information is supplied so the property can be easily identified by the Land Registrar. In addition, if a search is requested of property which is difficult to identify, a plan should be supplied with the application. This application is made by using Form 109 (Office Copy of the Register and Title Plan) and the cost is £4.00 for the Office Copy and £4.00 for a copy of the plan if required. The result of this search will then enable (if the land is registered) copies of the entries on the Register to be obtained and inspected. This information is particularly useful when considering enforcement by way of a charging order. A further development has also seen an opportunity for telephone service searches to be undertaken. The Chief Land Registrar has issued directions on this which speed up the information gathering process. There is a fee for this service of £8.00 per title and it is only available to those who hold credit accounts at the Land Registry (most solicitors do).

If a phone application is to be made, you do not phone the relevant District Land Registry, but the following telephone number (between 11.00 am and 4.00 pm): 0845 308 4545

Advice will then be given which individual Land Registry is dealing with the particular area. If the required Office Copy is not received, then contact must be made with the individual registry. Again, online Land Registry inquiries are available.

- Attachment of earnings index. This is kept pursuant to CCR Ord 27, r 2. The proper officer of every court keeps a nominal index of the debtors residing within the district of his court in respect of whom there are in force attachment of earnings orders which have been made by that court or of which the proper officer has received notice from another court. This index can be searched by any person having a judgment or order against a person believed to be residing within the district of the court and a certificate will be issued. If an attachment of earnings order is revealed, then consideration should be given to consolidating with this.

The standard form is Form N336 in the county court forms. No fee is payable.

- Register of Bills of Sale. This is a more specialised register. To be effective, all bills of sale must be registered at the Filing Department, Central Office, Royal Courts of Justice and if there is concern that certain assets may be subject to a bill of sale, a search should be done there. The fee for an official certificate of the result of a search in one name in any register or index number under the custody of the Register of Bills of Sale is £2.00 and for every additional name, if included in the same Certificate, an extra fee of £1.00.

- Insolvency. An up to date confirmation of whether or not a winding-up petition has been presented against the company can be obtained by telephoning the companies court (which keeps a central index of winding-up petitions). The relevant telephone number is (020) 7947 7328. In addition, a public terminal exists for searching the index of prior petitions in the Thomas More Building, Royal Courts of Justice, London. This search is of particular importance if a solicitor is contemplating winding-up proceedings. There is nothing more frustrating than sending off the papers duly issued to see them returned, because another creditor has already issued proceedings. This index obviously provides much more up to date information than the company search which will probably have been undertaken earlier.

Further, a manual index is maintained at the Royal Courts of Justice of administration petitions presented in the High Court (but not the county court).

For individuals, there is a register of bankruptcy notices and petitions kept at the Thomas More Building, but, as stated above, a search of the Land Charges Registry will reveal whether there is a pending bankruptcy (a registration preceded by the letters PA(B)) or if the bankruptcy order has been made (a registration preceded by the letters WO(B)).

3.2   Pre-action protocols

3.2.1   A new regime

One of the features of the new Civil Procedure Rules was the creation of a number of pre-action protocols. These were effectively a recommended procedure that parties should undertake prior to the commencement of proceedings. They were significant because compliance or non-compliance with these protocols could be taken into account by the court when giving directions for the management of proceedings and when making orders for costs. The first two protocols to be adopted were in respect of personal injury and clinical negligence.

3.2.2   Draft pre-action protocol for claims for a specific sum of money

Much work was undertaken by a Law Society working party to draft a debt recovery protocol which would then, it was hoped, come into force in the same way as the other protocols. Despite there being much publicity, in Autumn 2000, plans for such a protocol were put on hold by the Lord Chancellor's Department, which postponed the protocol because of the wide range of suggested debtor response times in consultation. Nevertheless, the principles that were set out in that protocol are good ones to be utilised by creditors seeking to obtain money and most solicitors will seek to utilise those principles in their letter before action.

In summary, the protocol in its draft form gave guidance to the claimant or his solicitor as to what should go in the letter of claim and a timetable (of not less than seven days) for the defendant to reply.

It also contained provisions for the parties to disclose documents that may be appropriate in seeking to resolve the issues prior to the issue of court proceedings and (although this surely will be rare) set out a procedure for either party to disclose and deal with any expert evidence prior to the issue of proceedings.

Whether or not this protocol will be resurrected in the future is unknown.

3.3   The letter before action

As stated above, most solicitors will wish to write a letter before action before proceeding to the court process. It is not wrong to issue proceedings immediately, but there is a risk (particularly since the Civil Procedure Rules have come into force) that a District Judge, upon hearing the matter and being told by the debtor that a letter before action has not been written, may disallow the interest or the costs which would normally be awarded. (CPR 44.3) For this reason, it is strongly advised a solicitor's letter is written and, in practice, the court will expect such a procedure to have been undertaken. One way to avoid this would be for the client to have written a letter before action, indicating that in default of hearing within a requisite time period (which should give a sufficient period for response and this is usually at least seven days), then matters will be placed in the hands of a solicitor and interest and costs will be added. Most solicitors, however, prefer that this letter is drafted themselves and a suggested precedent is set out below.

3.3.1 Sample letter before action

Dear Sirs,

Re: name of client

We represent (name of client) of (address of client) and have been instructed concerning the sum of £(amount of debt) that is outstanding and overdue for payment from yourselves, in respect of (nature of goods/service provided).

We must advise you that unless we receive your remittance or acceptable proposals for payment within the next seven days from the date of this letter, we are instructed to issue Court proceedings.

If this is necessary no doubt you will appreciate this could well result in the amount to be paid by you being increased with the fees, costs and interest that will be claimed in addition to the debt.

We are authorised to accept payment from henceforth on behalf of our clients. Your payment should therefore be made payable to this firm at this office and be accompanied by a stamped addressed envelope if a receipt is required.

We would advise against making payment by post in cash but if you choose to do so, that will be at your own risk.

If you require any further details we would ask that you contact us on (telephone number) quoting reference (solicitor's reference).

Yours faithfully

3.3.2 Points to note in the letter before action

Ensure the letter is correctly addressed. If pursuing a company, mark it for the attention of the director (name him or her if possible). There is a risk, however, in doing this if the director is away from the office and he is later able to show that it did not come to his attention within the stated time period. In this case, any future action could be delayed. If pursuing an individual, then again ensure the correct full name and address are utilised. If there is some doubt about these, basic checks either in the telephone directory or possibly with the Electoral Registration office may elicit some information.

If pursuing a partnership, it is better to sue the individuals rather than relying on the trade name of the partnership because of the more effective enforcement action available. This is another reason for ensuring that clients obtain the full names of all the partners. In this case, the letter before action should be addressed to the individuals quoting the partnership name, for example, John Smith and Hubert Brown (trading as Smith & Brown Painters and Decorators).

State clearly the name and address of your client and the amount of the debt. Often, invoice details are quoted, but this practice becomes complicated if the debt is made up of a number of invoices.

Make it clear that in default of payment within a requisite time period (normally seven, 10 or 14 days), proceedings will follow without further notice and will include claims for interest and costs.

It is considered good practice (and in the spirit of the new Civil Procedure Rules) to indicate a contact point and give the debtor an opportunity to contact the solicitors with a view to either discussing the matter or his proposals.

4 The Commencement of Proceedings

4.1 A new procedure

Prior to the Civil Procedure Rules, any book on debt recovery discussed in detail the differences in the county court and High Court jurisdictions and the advantages and disadvantages in pursuing cases in the particular courts. Matters have now become somewhat easier in that one single claim form has replaced the various forms that previously were used. Therefore, all proceedings commenced since 26 April 1999 must be commenced pursuant to the new procedure. Since this time, the person bringing the action is no longer called the plaintiff, but the claimant.

4.1.1 Consumer Credit Act claims

The Consumer Credit Act 1974 set out a new regime for dealing with such claims. The procedure is set out in the Practice Direction which supplements CPR 7.9.

In view of the specialised nature of these proceedings, this book will not deal with such claims in any detail and will concentrate on the standard debt recovery proceedings which occupy the vast majority of the courts' time.

4.2 High Court or county court

Although only one claim form is utilised, it is still necessary to consider the two courts both in respect of substantive proceedings and enforcement.

The following points are relevant:

4.2.1   Proceedings (whether for damages or for a specified sum) may not be started in the High Court unless the value of the claim is £15,000.00 or more (Practice Direction which supplements CPR Part 7) (in this regard, note that proceedings which include a claim for damages in respect of personal injury must not be started in the High Court unless the value of the claim is £50,000.00 or more).

In view of the importance of this Practice Direction, it is set out in part as at Appendix B.

Subject to the financial limited of £15,000.00, a claim should be started in the High Court if the financial value and the amount in dispute justifies it and/or the complexity of the facts, legal issues, remedies or procedures justify it and/or the claim has interest to the public in general rather than the claimant in particular.

There is provision in the CPR (Part 30) for the transfer of provisions between the High and county courts.

4.2.2   There are more efficient enforcement procedures available in the High Court as will be seen later.

4.2.3   Interest runs on all High Court judgments, but only runs on county court judgments where the sum involved is £5,000.00 or more (and even then certain types of judgment are excluded) pursuant to the County Courts (Interest on Judgment Debts) Order 1991 SI 1991/1184, which applies to all judgments subsequent to 1 July 1991.

4.2.4   Only county court judgments can be registered and this therefore may be an advantage in utilising the county court, as this can sometimes prompt payment, as it can affect the debtor's creditworthiness.

4.2.5   No attachment of earnings orders are available in the High Court (except for rare cases).

4.2.6   A simpler process of oral examination of the debtor exists in the county court.

4.2.7   Administration orders exist in the county court (but not the High Court), and for more information on this procedure, see CCR Ord 39 (which is included under CPR Sched 2).

4.3   Transfer of proceedings

Even prior to the Civil Procedure Rules, s 40 of the County Courts Act 1984 (as substituted by s 2(1) of the Courts and Legal Services Act 1990) improved the process of transfer between the two courts and was utilised to ensure that as far as possible, debt recovery actions took place in the county court. This process has been taken further by the Civil Procedure Rules (Part 30) and it is now highly unlikely that defended debt actions will take place in the High Court unless very substantial issues and sums of money are involved.

There is also provision in ss 41 and 42 of the County Courts Act 1984 for a transfer of county court proceedings to the High Court. However, this is rarely utilised in debt actions.

4.4   Interest

Reference has already been made to the importance of interest in debt proceedings. Indeed, the correct claiming of interest can result in considerable compensation for the client and it is incumbent upon practitioners to ensure that the principles and rules are correctly followed.

4.4.1 Preliminary points

The current rate of interest pursuant to the Judgment Debts (Rates of Interest) Order 1993 SI 1993/564 is 8%, with effect from 1 April 1993. This Order amended s 17 of the Judgments Act 1838 and reduces the interest from the previously artificially high level of 15% to 8% per annum.

The rate of 8% applies not only to interest on judgment debts, but is the relevant amount of interest to be claimed upon the issue of proceedings if no contractual interest is claimed, or interest is not claimed pursuant to the Late Payment of Commercial Debts (Interest) Act 1998 (see 4.4.4).

It should be remembered that the client's terms and conditions will normally allow for either seven days, 14 days, 28 days or one month for payment and, therefore, the interest calculation should be made from that date and not the date of invoice, unless the terms and conditions declare otherwise.

If the client's terms and conditions include contractual interest, then any claim must refer to that, although it may be advisable to refer to statutory interest in the alternative. Statutory interest in the High Court is based on s 35A of the Supreme Court Act 1981. Statutory interest in the county court is based on s 69 of the County Courts Act 1984.

4.4.2 Rules for claiming interest in a debt action

In order to ensure recovery in both the High Court and county court, interest must be claimed specifically: the amount of interest claimed must be shown and the rate at which, and the period for which, it is claimed. Failure to do this could mean that the court would disallow interest. Although it is always possible to apply at any date to amend the interest claimed, there could be penalisation in costs.

If dealt with correctly, a claim will show the amount of interest claimed, the number of days upon which it is claimed and the rate of interest up to the date of issue of proceedings, and thereafter it will plead a daily rate of interest from the date of issue of proceedings until judgment or sooner payment.

4.4.3 How to deal with the interest claim

If the claim has been started in the High Court, then not only must interest be set out in the body of the particulars of claim, but also at the end of the particulars of claim the following wording should be utilised with regard to interest (for the purposes of this example, it is assumed there is only one invoice and therefore one interest calculation):

AND the Claimant claims:

(1) the sum of (debt amount)

(2) ... interest on the sum claimed in para (1) above pursuant to s 35A of the Supreme Court Act 1981 at the rate of 8% per annum from the (date from which interest is claimed) to the date hereof being ... days.

(3) Interest on the sum claimed in para (1) hereof pursuant to s 35A of the Supreme Court Act 1981 at the rate of 8% per annum from the date hereof to the date of judgment or sooner payment which is a daily rate of ...

(4) Alternatively, interest claimed pursuant to s 35A of the Supreme Court Act 1981 on the amount claimed in para (1) hereof at such rate and for such period as the court may deem just.

The final clause is put in to cover the situation of there being an error in the interest calculation.

4.4.4 Examples of the interest claim

If proceedings have been commenced in the county court, then interest is claimed both in the main body of the particulars of claim pursuant to s 69 of the County Courts Act 1984 and again at the end of the particulars of claim. Hence, assuming one invoice and one interest calculation, the document will end as follows:

AND the Claimant claims

(1) the sum of (debt amount)

(2) ... interest on the sum claimed in para (1) above pursuant to s 69 of the County Courts Act 194 at the rate of 8% per annum from the (date from which interest is claimed), to the date hereof being ... days.

(3) Interest on the sum claimed in para (1) hereof pursuant to s 69 of the County Courts Act 1984 at the rate of 8% per annum from the date hereof to the date of judgment or sooner payment which is a daily rate of ...

(4) Alternatively, interest pursuant to s 69 of the County Courts Act 1984 on the amount claimed in para (1) hereof at such rate and for such period as the court may deem just.

4.4.5 Late Payment of Commercial Debts (Interest) Act 1998

It has already been seen that interest on monies that are owed can be claimed either pursuant to the contractual terms agreed between the parties or pursuant to s 35A of the Supreme Court Act 1981 or s 69 of the County Courts Act 1984 once proceedings are issued.

There is now a third way: interest can be claimed pursuant to the Late Payment of Commercial Debts (Interest) Act 1998.

This Act gives the right for parties in certain circumstances to claim interest, whether or not court proceedings are taken.

Currently, the first two phases of the Act are in force, which means that small businesses can claim interest from large businesses and the public sector or indeed from other small businesses.

On 1 November 2002, the Act will be widened to cover all businesses.

Pursuant to the Act, small businesses are defined as businesses with 50 or fewer employees on average over the previous financial year prior to the year the contract was made. The business can be a sole proprietorship, partnership or company.

Under the Act, if a business qualifies in the above circumstances, then if payment is not made within the agreed credit period (either through the contractual agreement or within the default period of 30 days), the party who has not been paid is entitled to claim interest at 8% over the Bank of England base rate at the end of the day on which the contract says that payment is to be made or, if no date is stipulated, at the end of the last day of the default period.

It may be advisable, if a party is able to claim such interest, for this sum to be set out in the claim form as an alternative interest claim.

At this time, initial research has not shown that this Act has been widely used, but the full effect will not be known until it is completely in force on 1 November 2002.

4.5   Costs

The Civil Procedure Rules (Part 45) lay down fixed costs upon the issue of proceedings in terms of costs to be paid and recoverable costs.

Reference should always be made to the current fees order as these costs are subject to amendment.

The claim form may include a claim for fixed commencement costs which are calculated by reference to a table set out in CPR 45.2 (see Appendix C).

In general terms, the higher the value of the claim, the higher the fixed fee and an additional fee is allowed for personal service of the claim form and if there is more than one defendant who is personally served.

In addition to these fixed costs, any appropriate court fee will be allowed in the final computation.

The most common fees for debt recovery, correct as at the date of publication, are set out in Chapter 17.

4.6   The claim form

The claim form replaces the old form of writ (High Court) and summons (county court) and applies to all proceedings issued on or after 26 April 1999. The procedure is fully laid out in CPR Part 7. To some extent, this new (combined) procedure simplifies matters, but there are one or two fundamental changes from the old practice.

The claim form is a relatively straightforward document and can be obtained from any law stationers or the county court (or is available over the Internet). It is helpfully given the number N1.

Pursuant to CPR 7.2(1), proceedings are started when the court issues a claim form at the request of the claimant and the issue date is the one that is entered on the form by the court.

The claim form will either contain the particulars of claim themselves which are served with it or the concise statement of that claim with the particulars of claim themselves to follow (within 14 days after service of the claim form) (CPR 7.4).

Pursuant to the tenor of the Civil Procedure Rules and Lord Woolf's reforms, more informal and less wordy particulars of claim can be utilised providing that the defendant has a clear understanding of what is being claimed against him.

4.6.1 Statement of value

CPR Part 16 gives further information on statements of case and by CPR 16.3, the claimant must in the claim form either state the amount of money which he is claiming or that he expects to recover to be either not more than £5,000.00; more than £5,000.00, but not more than £15,000.00; or more than £15,000.00. This 'statement of value' is to assist the court in considering upon which track the claim should be allocated but, of course, in the vast majority of debt recovery actions, it will be possible to say exactly what is being claimed.

4.6.2 Interest

As has already been seen, interest is an important part of debt recovery proceedings and CPR 16.4(2) sets out what is required by way of claiming interest.

4.6.3 Statement of truth

This is a new development under the Civil Procedure Rules and pursuant to CPR Part 22 the particulars of claim must be verified by a statement of truth. Detailed rules with regard to these statements of truth are laid out in CPR Part 22 and effectively utilised in the vast majority of court documents which set out a claimant and defendant's case in a debt recovery action.

A detailed Practice Direction supports Part 22 but, in respect of the particulars of claim, the statement of truth that must be annexed to that document must be as follows:

> (I believe)(The claimant believes) that the facts stated in these particulars of claim are true.

This statement must then be signed by either the claimant or his legal representative (or a litigation friend).

Because such statements could constitute a contempt of court if dishonestly given, most solicitors will request that their client signs the document or (at the very least) will obtain an indemnity from the client before signing themselves. It is suggested that the best practice is to ensure the client signs the document and at the same time, of course, checks the veracity of the same. One consequence of this is that it may mean that there is a further slight delay before proceedings are issued if documents have to be considered and signed by the clients. Due provision should be made for this when calculating the interest claim and when planning the case itself.

4.6.4 Lodging the claim form and supporting documents at court

Once the claim form and supporting documentation have been duly checked and signed, it is lodged at court. There is no restriction on which court is used and, therefore, the claimant will usually seek to issue proceedings in the court that is either his own 'home court' or that of his solicitors. Two copies of the claim form (if there is only one defendant) are lodged (always ensure that one copy is also kept for the solicitor's file) and the relevant court fee in force at the time is also lodged at court. Those court fees vary depending on the amount in issue and a list correct as at the date of publication is set out in Chapter 17.

In the vast majority of cases, the claimant asks the court to serve the claim form although if the claimant wishes to serve the form himself or through his solicitors, then a request can be made of the court when lodging the documents.

4.6.5 Bulk production centre

Some heavy court users (often banks or utilities or specialist debt recovery solicitors) utilise the production centre for the issue of claim forms and their court process. Provision for this is made in the CPR 7.10 and for bulk users of court service, the opportunities presented and the service offered should be seriously considered. Further information about this process can be obtained from The County Court Bulk Centre, St Catherines House, 4th Floor, Northampton. The Claims Production Centre Code of Practice and the County Court Bulk Centre Rules of Membership which outline what is done and how it is done can be obtained by telephoning (01604) 609 506.

4.7 The correct defendant

Again, the importance of full information to establish the identity of the correct defendant becomes relevant here and the importance of the client questionnaire referred to earlier cannot be over-stressed. The three most common situations in debt recovery are clearly the pursuing of an individual, a partnership or a company.

4.7.1 The individual defendant

Providing the correct full name and current address is known, there are no special rules to follow. If the debt is a joint and several one (for example, a joint bank account for a husband and wife), then both should be named as defendants.

4.7.2 A partnership

Ensure first of all that your client is sure he is dealing with a partnership and not a limited company. Reference should be made to RSC Ord 81 and CCR Ord 5, r 9. The advantage of suing the partners as individuals, rather than solely in the firm's name is that if a judgment is obtained against a partnership name then leave must subsequently be obtained to enforce against the assets of the individual partners. In certain cases, it may be difficult, of course, to find the identity of the individual or individuals, but assistance may be obtained from the Business Names Act 1985. This provides a requirement for disclosure of names of partners and, in relation to each person so named, an address in Great Britain at which service of any document relating in any way to the business will be effective. These names must be stated on all business letters, written orders for goods or services to be supplied to the business, invoices and receipts issued in the course of the business and written demands for the payments of debts arising in the course of the business.

In addition, at any premises where the business is carried on, there must be displayed in a prominent position a notice containing such names and addresses.

There was previously a Registry of Business Names, but that is no longer operative.

Furthermore, once proceedings have been issued, a claimant is able to make a formal demand, if proceedings have been issued against a partnership, for the names of the individual partners and their places of residence. This request must be complied with by the partnership and all names and addresses must be given of those who were partners in the firm when the cause of the action arose (see RSC Ord 81, r 2 and CCR Ord 5, r 9(2)).

4.7.3 The corporate defendant

The full and correct name and the current registered office of a company will have been obtained from a search at Companies House (the details revealed by this procedure have been referred to in Chapter 2), but it is always advisable just before issuing proceedings to check that the company has not been wound up or is not subject to any form of insolvency process. Any company agents should be able to tell you that information, or alternatively, enquiries can be made , as previously stated, at Companies House or at the Companies Court. It is clearly frustrating both for a solicitor and his client to issue proceedings and then to find that a company has already been put into liquidation. It should of course be remembered that the liquidation of a company effectively stays the legal process that is being pursued.

The check referred to in 2.2.5 by telephone inquiry of the Companies Court should also be made as close to the issue of proceedings as is possible.

Although it is appropriate to serve at the registered office address, it is now permissible to serve at a business address or an address connected with the business (CPR Part 6).

4.8   Service of proceedings

There are the following possibilities of service of proceedings:
* personal service;
* postal service (first class post);
* leaving the document at a specified place;
* service through a document exchange;
* service by fax or other means of electronic communication.

These methods of service are all set out in CPR Part 6. In addition, the new Civil Procedure Rules do not remove any of the methods that are set out in the Companies Act for serving companies.

Although at first glance, this would not be a great change from the position that previously existed, in the vast majority of cases, all proceedings will now be served by the court and, therefore, in the main proceedings will be served by first class post. It should be remembered that service is by first class post and not recorded delivery. Service by post is, however, fraught with uncertainty and professional debtors may be able to promote appropriate delays by claiming never to have received the proceedings.

For this reason, personal or 'letter box' service (by leaving the document at a specified place) is an attractive option and promotes certainties. If this is to be followed, then the solicitors should request that the proceedings are returned to them by the court for service. Under previous rules, there were the opportunities to obtain an order for 'substituted service' and pursuant to CPR 6.8, the courts have the power to authorise service by other method if there is 'good reason' so to do.

4.8.1 Service on solicitors

If it is possible to persuade solicitors to accept service, then this clearly promotes certainty. However, most solicitors acting for defendants in debt recovery cases will not be prepared to accept service. If, however, they do, then the claimant's solicitor must send written confirmation of the acceptance by the defendant's solicitors and request the court to serve the solicitors in a covering letter.

4.8.2 Electronic means of service

Although, in theory, this seems to be a very innovative move by the courts, the Practice Direction which supplements CPR Part 6 makes it clear that detailed circumstances will have to be followed before service by either fax or other electronic means can be deemed to be effective. In summary, there must be an acceptance by the party or his legal representative (on a previous occasion) that service by this method can follow and a provision of fax or electronic mail address.

Some concern has been voiced by solicitors as to whether having a fax number on their notepaper would open the floodgates to the such proceedings. In this regard, the practice direction supplementing CPR

Part 6 does state that a fax number on the notepaper is a written indication of a willingness to accept service by fax. For this reason, it is not unusual to find an exclusion as to the acceptance of any proceedings by fax or email on solicitors' notepaper.

4.8.3 Place of service

CPR 6.5(6) sets out the places for service for particular defendants as follows:

- individual – usual or last known residence;
- proprietor of business – usual or last known residence or place of business or last known place of business;
- individual who is suing or being sued in the name of a firm – usual or last known residence or principal or last known place of business of the firm;
- company registered in England and Wales – principal office of the company or any place of company within the jurisdiction which has a real connection with the claim.

4.8.4 Computation of time of service of proceedings

CPR 6.7(1) sets out the dates of deemed service for the different methods of service as follows:

- first class post – the second day after it was posted;
- document exchange – the second day after it was left at the document exchange;
- delivering the document to or leaving it at a permitted address – the day after it was delivered to or left at the permitted address;
- fax – if it is transmitted on a business day before 4.00 pm, on that day or in any other case, on the business day after the day on which it is transmitted;
- other electronic method – the second day after the day on which it is transmitted.

It is perhaps ironic that electronic method (deemed to be instantaneous communication) is not necessarily deemed to be so by the Civil Procedure Rules.

4.8.5 What if the defendant resides out of the jurisdiction?

Complicated and detailed rules apply for service out of the jurisdiction and depending upon the particular circumstances of the defendant and the country involved, reference should be made to CPR 6.19–6.31 and the supporting Practice Direction.

4.9 The response pack

Once proceedings have been successfully issued at court, then (subject to the method of service), the defendant will be served with a response pack which will be made up of:

- the claim form;
- an acknowledgment of service;
- a defence and counterclaim form;
- a form of admission.
- also contained within the package are detailed notes which set out the procedure that is to be adopted in the proceedings that have been served.

5 The Continuation of the Legal Action

The purpose of this chapter is to indicate how effective and swift action with use of the relevant Civil Procedure Rules can ensure that a successful recovery of a debt is obtained for clients. Other Practice Notes in this series deal with the progress of a defended action. Inevitably, the vast majority of debt actions conclude without the need for a full trial. If early judgment cannot be obtained and a full trial is necessary, then a more detailed analysis than this Practice Note permits will be necessary from the appropriate text.

5.1 Judgment in default

Court proceedings for debt recovery are by their nature for a fixed sum (together with interest and costs) and, therefore, practitioners do not need to concern themselves with judgment for damages to be assessed. Instead, application can be made for a judgment in default of the defendant stating the particular matter is to be defended.

5.2 The legal framework

Reference has already been made to the service of proceedings and the different ways this can be effected (see Chapter 4) and a defendant who wishes to defend a claim brought against him must respond to the claim within appropriate time periods or risk a judgment being obtained against him by default.

As has already been seen, he will be sent together with the claim, 'a response pack' which, helpfully, will also include some notes and guidance for him.

If the particulars of claim have not been served with the claim form, then the defendant need not respond until they are served on him (CPR 9.1(2)).

If, however, particulars of claim are served with the claim form or within the 14 day period allowed after service, then the defendant must respond in accordance with CPR 9.2 and either:

• file or serve an admission in accordance with CPR Part 14 or;

• file a defence in accordance with CPR Part 15 (or do both, if he admits any part of the claim); or

• file an acknowledgment of service in accordance with CPR Part 10.

There are strict time periods pursuant to which the defendant must act, namely, the defendant must file at court either his defence or the acknowledgment of service within 14 days after service of the particulars of claim and it has already been seen in Chapter 4 how the dates of service are calculated.

5.2.1 The acknowledgment of service

The procedure for dealing with an acknowledgment of service is set out in CPR Part 10.

If the defendant chooses to complete the acknowledgment of service, then effectively he gains a further 14 day period before he has to file his defence or dispute the jurisdiction of the court (CPR 10.1).

If no acknowledgment of service or a defence is filed within the 14 day period after service of the claim form, then judgment in default maybe obtained (CPR 10.2).

A Practice Direction which supplements CPR Part 10 sets out the way the acknowledgment of service is to be completed, but it is a simple form and does not promote any difficulties. If the defendant is legally represented then, normally, that legal representative would sign the form. If the defendant is a company, then the Practice Direction permits the person 'holding a senior position in the company or corporation' to sign the acknowledgment of service on the defendant's behalf, but he must state the position he holds. Normally, of course, this would be a director or other officer of the company.

Where the defendant is a partnership, the acknowledgment of service may be signed by any of the partners or a person having the control or management of the partnership business.

5.2.2 Disputing the courts' jurisdiction

In rare cases, the defendant may state in the acknowledgment of service that he is going to dispute the courts' jurisdiction and, if so, CPR Part 11 comes into play. This would be an extremely unusual situation in debt recovery actions, as this particular provision is provided by the rules to cover the possibility of the matter being dealt with by arbitration or if there is a conflict of laws situation whereby the defendant may be seeking to say that the case should be dealt with by another legal jurisdiction. If this procedure is to be followed, then CPR Part 11 sets out the procedure that must be undertaken after the acknowledgment of service has been filed. In essence, the procedure must be undertaken within a 14 day period when the defence would be filed and evidence must be supplied in support.

5.2.3 Admitting the claim

It should not be forgotten that there may not be a defence to the claim and that position is acknowledged by the defendant. If this is the case, then the response pack that is sent to the defendant gives him the opportunity to admit the claim pursuant to CPR Part 14 and to complete the admission form that is included in the pack. As debt recovery proceedings will invariably be for a specified sum, the form to be completed is Form N9A.

If the defendant wishes to admit part of the claim and defend the rest he is able to do that by completing both the admission form and the defence form included in the pack. Again the time period to complete these forms is the standard fourteen days after service of the claim form.

Once this admission form is filed at court then the claimant may proceed to obtain judgment pursuant to CPR 14.1(4).

Obtaining judgment by this route is of course a 'paper exercise' and the judgment is for the whole amount of the debt (or the amount that has been admitted) together with interest and the fixed costs, providing of course interest has been correctly claimed (CPR 14.14).

It should be remembered that if there has been an admission of part of the claim but the defendant wants to defend the balance, then if the claimant accepts the part admission, he may not then continue to proceed with the defended element. It may well be the case, therefore, that careful commercial decisions will have to be made if this situation occurs.

Often, in cases of an admission, the defendant, whilst realising there is no defence to the claim, requests time to make payment and this request is filed with the admission (CPR 14.9).

The claimant is informed of the request for time to pay and if he accepts the proposal, then the judgment will be made on those terms pursuant to the request of the claimant.

If the proposal is not accepted, then the claimant informs the court and a court officer will make an administrative decision upon the rate of payment (CPR 14.11) and inform the parties. Either party may then apply pursuant to CPR 14.13 for a redetermination by a District Judge.

The whole basis of this procedure is to deal with proceedings in as swift a way as possible for both parties.

5.2.4 Judgment in default of defence

It has already been seen that an acknowledgment of service will gain further time for a defendant, but if a defence is not filed in the 14 day period after filing of the acknowledgment of service, then the claimant is entitled to apply for judgment in default. Similarly, if the acknowledgment of service is not filed within that initial 14 day period, the claimant can at that stage move to obtain a judgment by default.

The procedure is set out at CPR Part 12.

The procedure is again a simple one and no court fee has to be paid. The claimant will be advised to check with the court at the expiry of the relevant time period that no documents have been lodged direct at court and not forwarded, but if nothing has been filed, then he simply completes Form N225, claiming the full claim together with interest to the date of judgment (which can be calculated exactly on the form) together with the court fees on the claim and the solicitors' costs on the claim and the further solicitors' costs that are allowed on entering judgment. It should also be noted that many courts, as a matter of convenience, will issue to a claimant Form N205A, which is a combined notice of issue (specifying amount) and a request for judgment, so this form can be used if judgment is sought at the appropriate time.

It is open for the claimant to request that the judgment is paid by instalments, but this is not a step that should be undertaken and it is much better to ensure the claimant is in the driving seat by requesting that judgment is obtained for the whole amount to be payable immediately.

The amount of costs that are allowed are set out in CPR 45.4 and do vary depending on the circumstances and the amount that is owed. Care should be taken to ensure that the most up to date cost figures are utilised (see Appendix C).

5.3   A defended debt action

5.3.1 Introduction

If the defendant to a debt action does file a defence and/or counterclaim, then the case is ready to proceed as a defended action and, as stated earlier, the scope of a fully defended action is not part of the remit of this book.

It may be, however, that the defence filed is in such a form that it is clear that it is not a true defence to the claim and, in these circumstances, the claimant must decide whether he wishes to 'short circuit' the full trial and apply pursuant to CPR Part 24 for summary judgment.

It should also be mentioned that one of the very positive features of the new Rules is that they enable the court to intervene and strike out claims or defences if they are clearly untenable.

There are a number of opportunities when the court can consider the case of its own initiative and make orders and, in practice, the parties have been surprised under the new Rules at the extent to which their cases have been dealt with in this manner. This is a fundamental change, since under the previous procedure, it was very much up to the parties to drive the litigation forward. This intervention by the courts is a recognition of the fact that litigation is now very much 'court and Judge driven'.

A District Judge, therefore, could decide that the defence that has been filed is not really a defence at all and strike it out at any early stage (CPR Part 3.4). It should be noted that this rule applies equally to claimants' statements of case as to defendants' defences.

On the assumption, however, that the debt recovery claim has been properly brought, if the defendant wants to pursue a defence, he must ensure that his defence is properly set out and reference should be made to CPR 16.5.

Prior to the changes, defendants often tried to 'buy time' by simply lodging a 'bare denial'. The person bringing the claim would then have to make an application for summary judgment on the grounds that this was not a true defence. Such a defence would now in many cases be automatically struck out by the court without the need for the claimant to bring a summary judgment application.

5.4 Summary judgment

Under the old rules of court, summary judgment was obtainable (although not for small claims).

CPR Part 24 and the Practice Direction that supplements it sets out the way this procedure proceeds.

The claimant can make his application for summary judgment once an acknowledgment of service has been filed (and before the defence is received) but, of course, if he does that, then the defendant will not have to file a defence until the application is determined. If, therefore, the claimant does not believe there is a defence, he has to make an informed decision with his legal advisor as to whether or not he would be best placed to wait 14 days and see if a defence is filed (and, if not, enter judgment by default) or move forward with a summary judgment application (which will probably not be heard until a few weeks later).

It is, of course, open for the claimant to make his application for summary judgment once a defence has been filed if he does not believe it is a proper defence.

As stated earlier, summary judgment did not used to be available in 'small claims'. That has now changed and the remedy is freely available.

5.4.1 Summary judgment claim procedure

For the purposes of this description, it will be assumed that the claimant is the party that is making the application for summary judgment, but it should not be forgotten that under the new Rules, it is quite open for a defendant to seek to remove what he considers to be an unmeritorious claim by seeking a 'summary judgment'.

Whether a claimant or defendant is bringing the application to court, the test is the same, namely that it is for the party bringing the application to show that the other party has no real prospect of success in the action.

This represents a further subtle change from the old Rules, in that defendants would normally successfully prevent summary judgment being obtained against them if they could show that they had a 'arguable' case. Under the new Rules, it is now a harder test to satisfy to prevent summary judgment being obtained and, therefore, it follows that more summary judgment applications should be successful (whether by claimant or defendant).

To make an application, the claimant would complete Form N244 (the Application Notice) but, pursuant to the Practice Direction that supplements CPR Part 24, that Application Notice must include a statement that it is an application for summary judgment under Part 24 and either the notice or the evidence contained or referred to in it or served with it must:

- identify concisely any point of law or provision in a document on which the applicant relies; and/or

- a statement must be made that the applicant believes that on the evidence, the respondent has no real prospect of succeeding on the claim or issue or (as the case may be) of successfully defending the claim or the issue to which the application relates; and

- in either case, state that the applicant knows of no other reason why the disposal of the claim or issue should await trial.

Sometimes, the summary judgment application notice itself may contain all the evidence on which the applicant relies but, if not, that application notice must identify the written evidence on which he relies.

It is then for the respondent to file written evidence if he wishes to rely on any and serve that at least seven days before the summary judgment hearing (the application notice makes this clear).

There is a final opportunity for the applicant to rely on written evidence in reply and file and serve that at least three days before the hearing.

In summary judgment applications, evidence is by way of witness statements.

Under CPR 24.6, there are various outcomes of a summary judgment application, in that the court could:

- give judgment for the party seeking that judgment;
- strike out or dismiss a pleading;

- dismiss the application itself and give directions as to the filing and service of a defence and further directions about the management of the case;
- make a conditional order.

5.4.2 Conditional orders

These were, of course, often seen in previous cases when the party on the end of a summary judgment application would only be allowed to continue to defend the proceedings if a sum of money was paid into court or further steps taken. Such conditional orders are retained under the new rules (CPR 3.1(3)).

5.5   The defended debt action beyond summary judgment

If a party successfully overcomes the summary judgment application, then the case proceeds as a defended action. The continuance of such an action is beyond the scope of this book, but it should be noted that the Civil Procedure Rules revolutionised the way actions were to proceed, with a view to making justice speedier, more user friendly and more in tune with the modern way of life. At the heart of these new rules, therefore, is the introduction of an interventionist approach by the courts who will take the management of a case onto themselves and seek to dictate the time table to the parties.

As the essence of a successful solicitor in the area of debt recovery is speed of response, the Rules should assist those seeking to collect money.

A further consequence of this procedure is that it may bring about quicker negotiated settlements rather than under the old system, when negotiations often did not proceed successfully until the parties were about to commence trial.

5.6   Encouraging settlement

Another of Lord Woolf's tenets of the new Civil Procedure Rules was the use of mediation, alternative dispute resolution and other methods of encouraging settlement.

If a debt recovery case has not been disposed of by way of early judgment, then it will be allocated to one of the three tracks: small claims (in general terms, up to £5,000.00); fast track (in general terms, up to £15,000.00) and multitrack (other claims). This allocation is undertaken by the court considering allocation questionnaires completed by the parties, but one of the first questions on that particular document is whether or not the parties wish there to be stay for a one month period in order to facilitate attempts to settle (CPR 26.4). The allocation questionnaire which is now utilised as part of this process is a new stage in debt recovery and all litigation.

Furthermore, as the overriding objective of the new Rules is to deal with cases 'justly', this will include saving expense and therefore encouraging mediation or alternative dispute resolution. If a party is not prepared to explore these possibilities, then there could be an adverse finding in respect of costs at the end of the case. Any practitioner in this field, therefore, must consider whether a client's case is to be served by seeking to negotiate through any of these methods and bear in mind, of course, that from a client's point of view, it is not how the result is obtained, but whether money is recovered that is the fundamental test.

6 Enforcement of a Judgment

6.1 Introduction

It is now assumed for the purposes of this book that a judgment has been obtained either through a defendant's default or through prompt and efficient use of the Civil Procedure Rules. Clearly, however, the obtaining of the judgment may only be the beginning of the claimant's attempt to recover money and the most important part of debt recovery work for a solicitor is the enforcing of that judgment. Several of the following chapters consider the major methods of enforcement which can be undertaken, both in the High Court and county court. It should be borne in mind, however, that the initial instructions which were taken from the client will remain just as important at the enforcement stage as, hopefully, all relevant information for efficient enforcement will already be on the solicitor's file.

6.2 Choosing the correct method of enforcement

It is too easy following the obtaining of a judgment to think that the difficult work has been done and simply to instruct the Sheriff to attend to seize goods (in the High Court) or the Bailiff (in the county court). Unfortunately, if these steps are undertaken without a consideration of all the circumstances of the debtor, then the client may not be best protected and it may simply be a case of further fees being incurred without appropriate recovery.

It is important, therefore, to take stock of the situation and to consider each of the major methods of enforcement, to decide which method is likely to be the most successful for the particular circumstances of the case.

The major methods of enforcement of a judgment are as follows:

High Court

- A writ of *fieri facias* (Sheriff's Execution).
- Charging order.
- Garnishee order.
- Equitable execution (the appointment of a Receiver).
- Sequestration.
- Bankruptcy and corporate winding-up.

County court

- Warrant of execution.
- Charging order.
- Garnishee order.
- Attachment of earnings order.
- The appointment of a Receiver.
- Judgment summons.
- Bankruptcy and corporate winding-up.

In addition, in both the High Court and county courts, a procedure for the oral examination of the debtor exists.

It will be noted from the above that there is no equivalent power in the High Court to the county court's powers to make an attachment of earnings order (though the judgment may be transferred to the county court) or to issue a judgment summons (except in family cases). The county court has no power equivalent to the writ of sequestration.

It will also immediately be noted that although civil procedure has to a large extent been codified into one regime under the Civil Procedure Rules, the separate procedures of the High Court and county court currently remain for enforcement. To that extent, the Rules of the Supreme Court (RSC) and County Court Rules (CCR) must still be utilised for enforcement purposes.

Previously, these Rules were to be found in the White Book for the High Court (now renamed Civil Procedure) and the Green Book for the county court (now renamed the Civil Court Practice). Both these books contain the enforcement rules and care should be taken to ensure the most up to date edition is utilised. Further, as has already been stated, by Sched 1 and Sched 2 to the Civil Procedure Rules, the RSC and

CCR which remain are set out and these include of course the enforcement rules.

6.3 Reform of enforcement law

Despite the major Civil Procedure reforms, there has not yet been a reform of the enforcement process. Many feel that is now necessary and to that end the Lord Chancellor's Department announced in March 1998 that it was initiating a comprehensive review of the enforcement of civil court judgments.

A consultation paper was published and has been further developed over the subsequent two years. As yet, there has not been any formal change to the law, but when the consultation process was commenced, it was envisaged that any changes would come into effect in late 2001. Information concerning this consultation paper and resulting developments can be found at the Lord Chancellor's website: **http://www.open.gov.uk/lcd/consult/general/enforce.htm**

6.4 High Court or county court enforcement?

It is often forgotten by practitioners that although a debt judgment may have been obtained in the county court, it is possible in certain circumstances to enforce through the High Court. In addition, any High Court judgment or order for any sum may be enforced through a county court (s 40 of the County Courts Act 1984), although it is difficult to envisage circumstances in which this would be appropriate, apart perhaps from a creditor seeking an Attachment of Earnings Order.

More important, therefore, is the power to transfer a county court judgment or order to the High Court. This procedure is set out in s 42 of the County Courts Act 1984 (as amended by the Courts and Legal Services Act 1990). The procedural requirements are set out in CCR Ord 25, r 13, and also developed in The Senior Masters Practice Direction of 31 August 1998 [1998] 4 All ER 63, which is set out at Appendix D.

Where proceedings for the enforcement of any judgment or order of a county court are transferred in this way, then the judgment or order maybe enforced as if it was a judgment or order of the High Court and it is treated as such.

The following points should be noted:

- There must be a judgment or order for the payment of a sum of money which has been given to the county court. Further, because of Art 8 of the High Court and County Court Jurisdiction Order 1991 SI 1991/724 (as amended by the High Court and County Court Jurisdiction (Amendment) Order 1999 SI 1999/1014) where it is sought to enforce the county court judgment wholly or partially by execution against goods then the amount involved must be greater than £600.00.

- In addition, in the same way, enforcement by execution for £5,000.00 or more may take place only in the High Court unless that judgment is pursuant to a Consumer Credit Act agreement.

Therefore, even if the sum is between £600.00 and £5,000.00, interest will continue to run after judgment (unlike in the county court). It will carry interest from the date of transfer.

6.4.1 Procedure for enforcement in the High Court of county court judgments

This procedure is set out in CCR Ord 25, r 13 (as amended) and also by the Practice Direction referred to above.

The procedure is as follows:

- A request is made to the proper officer of the court for a certificate of judgment.

- The certificate must state that it is granted 'for the purposes of enforcing the judgment (or order) in the High Court'. The certificate is signed by an officer of the issuing court.

- The certificate must comply with CCR Ord 22, r 8(1A). This certificate is then presented to the judgment counter clerk and it will be dated and sealed. No fee is payable for registration.

Thereafter, the judgment is treated as a High Court judgment and for all major forms of execution, reference should be made in the documentation to the fact that the judgment has been transferred. The title of all subsequent documents shall refer to the transfer in the title.

Upon transfer, of course, the judgment can be enforced with the generally more speedy methods of enforcement available in the High Court.

6.4.2 Sheriff's Lodgement Centre

If a judgment is either obtained in the High Court or transferred to the High Court for enforcement, then, in both cases, utilisation of the Sheriff's Lodgement Centre will be advantageous. This relatively new development is considered in detail in Chapter 8.

6.5 Immediate enforcement or oral examination?

If full information is not known about the debtor, then many practitioners would advise that an oral examination of the debtor takes place before the court. This is, in essence, a procedure whereby the debtor is examined on oath as to his means, assets and liabilities and a sworn document is produced which, hopefully, will produce more information for the claimant to be able to seek to enforce his judgment more efficiently.

The disadvantage is that this procedure can be a slow and cumbersome one. Many debtors do not attend upon the first hearing, and only on the second or third hearing, when the threat of a committal to prison for contempt of court is unleashed, is any information brought to the creditor's attention.

This procedure could, therefore, take several months, and indeed may well be a costly one, both in money and in chances of recovery of the debt for the creditor.

If the solicitor and client have worked together closely, then the information that an oral examination would reveal should, at least in part, be readily available.

For this reason, due consideration of all the facts of the case should be given before embarking on this procedure (a more detailed analysis is set out in Chapter 7). The relevant provisions are RSC Ord 48, r 1 and CCR Ord 25, r 3. If a judgment has been obtained against a limited company, it is possible to utilise this procedure to orally examine a director or other officer of that company.

6.6 Obtaining priority over other creditors

It is not unusual, of course, for several creditors to be chasing the same debtor (both corporate and individual).

6.6.1 Company searches

If dealing with a corporate debtor, an up to date company search to reveal whether or not an Administrative Receiver or Liquidator has been appointed could save time and expense (although not necessarily bring good news for the client). Alternatively, by telephoning the Companies Court (on (020) 7947 7328), information could be obtained as to the presentation of a winding-up petition. Even if information is revealed to this effect, the opportunity exists for the creditor to give a notice of intention to support the petition and it may also be possible to 'stand in the shoes' of the petitioning creditor if he or she is paid prior to the hearing of the petition. Reference should be made to the Insolvency Act 1986 and the Insolvency Rules issued with the Act for full details of this procedure.

6.6.2 Land charges searches

These searches at the Land Charges Registry may reveal whether or not any bankruptcy or charging orders are pending or have been made against the individual, as well as revealing further information.

Once the official search has been received, it is possible to obtain office copies of any of the entries which will complete the picture.

6.6.3 Search at the land registry

As has already been seen, a search of the Public Index Map Register will reveal whether the property consists of registered land or not and also provide, if this is the case, a title number.

It is then possible to obtain office copies of the register and this is useful and necessary information in relation to seeking to enforce a judgment by a charging order (see Chapter 9).

6.6.4 Working together

If other creditors are in a similar position against a debtor and are considering enforcement, then there may be merit in agreeing to work together and reach an agreement about payment of any funds recovered between the relevant parties and the sharing of solicitors' costs. Although there may be a saving in cost through this method, the disadvantages are, of course, that there will be other creditors who will be sharing the monies recovered.

6.6.5 Swift enforcement

In all debt recovery matters, swift action is required, but if creditors are aware of others seeking to recover money from the same debtor, then it is even more important that a prompt decision is undertaken and efficient enforcement undertaken. If it is known that property is owned (either by the debtor on his own or jointly with his spouse), then the speed of obtaining charging orders over the property could be the difference between recovering and not recovering money for a client.

7 The Oral Examination

7.1 Purpose of this procedure

Both the High Court and the county court have power to order a judgment debtor to attend before the court to be orally examined as to means, liabilities, assets and circumstances. This power exists not only with regard to an individual but, if the judgment debtor is a company, it enables an officer of the company to be orally examined on the company's behalf.

It is a procedure that is often utilised to enable a decision to be taken upon the correct method of enforcement, but, as has already been said, it could delay the efficient enforcement of a judgment.

Accordingly, a solicitor and his client must balance the advantage of hopefully obtaining more information against the disadvantage of the probable delays accompanying this procedure. Having said that, the fees are comparatively low and, in the long term, probably less than would be paid for other enforcement processes.

The practice and procedure varies from court to court and, therefore, it is advisable if conducting an examination in a court outside a solicitor's normal practice area to inquire how the local court requires the proceedings to be carried out. It is normally undertaken in private by an Officer of the Court. Sometimes, however, some courts will send out a questionnaire for the defendant to fill in first. If there is a particular examination where the solicitor feels that he or his client should be present, check with the local court as to the procedure to be adopted.

Normally, if no representative is present, then a copy of the answers will be sent to the claimant or his solicitor if his solicitor is on the court record, provided a letter has first been sent to the court requesting that an Officer of the Court conducts the examination. However, occasionally, courts will insist that a representative attends for the claimant.

As long ago as the late nineteenth century the courts made it clear that this procedure was to be taken seriously by debtors and in *Republic of Costa Rica v Strouberg* (1880) 16 Ch D 8, the court stated that the purpose of the procedure was 'not only to be an examination, but to be a cross-examination, and that the severest kind'. Unfortunately, many doubt the applicability of that statement to such proceedings today.

The relevant court will have its own form or questionnaire. Solicitors themselves often prepare forms by way of 'means questionnaires' either to seek to obtain information voluntarily without the need for an oral examination or as *aide memoire* for the information that they will be looking for when they receive the oral examination report. Such questionnaires of course should not be slavishly followed and information discovered at an oral examination may promote further lines of enquiry either at that examination or afterwards.

The debtor is asked to ensure that all relevant books, documents, accounts, evidence of liabilities, evidence of third party claims and hire purchase claims are produced as required by the court order. If the debtor fails to produce these documents, then an adjournment may be requested to enable them to be produced and the debtor should be asked to pay the cost of the adjournment (in fact, the court will probably only award nominal costs).

7.2　Procedure

7.2.1　The High Court

Historically, the High Court procedure for an oral examination was always more cumbersome than the county court procedure and the application always used to have to be made *ex parte* by affidavit. With the coming into force of the CPR, the perceived view is that an affidavit should no longer be insisted upon and, pursuant to the Practice Direction supplementing the CPR, Part 22, it is submitted that the application now can be made by satisfying the court that there is an unpaid judgment which is to be enforced. In accordance with the new procedure, therefore, this information could be given by witness statement containing the statement of truth which is an essential part of the new Rules.

Relevant forms and assistance can be obtained from Queens Bench Master's Practice Direction No 37 and Practice Forms (PF Nos 98 and 99).

The affidavit or witness statement is sent to the District Registry in which the judgment was obtained. Once the order has been obtained and duly sealed, it should be sent by the solicitor to the most convenient court for the debtor, which is usually the county court for the district in which the debtor resides, together with a request in letter form that the oral examination takes place there. This is so even if the judgment remains in the High Court. The county court will then insert the date of the appointment and return it to the solicitor for personal service on the debtor. When serving the order, travelling expenses for the debtor to and from the court must be paid or at least offered, even if refused.

Non-attendance at the hearing could entitle the creditor to seek an order for committal of the debtor (but see 7.2.2 below and references to the N39 procedure).

As in most court actions, any costs to be awarded by the court are at the court's discretion, but these would normally be awarded if it can be shown that there was merit in the oral examination from the creditor's point of view. If costs are allowed, they are endorsed upon the order with the direction that they are added to the judgment debt. Costs of personal service, plus the issue fee, plus costs for attendance can be claimed.

7.2.2 County court

This procedure is set out in CCR Ord 25, r 3 and was amended with effect from 2 May 2000. It consists of an application being made to the District Judge of the court in which the debtor resides or carries on business (there is no need for an affidavit).

Because the application is made to the court in which the debtor resides or carries on business, it may be the case that the judgment itself first has to be transferred to that court.

This transfer can be undertaken by writing a simple letter to the court where judgment was made, requesting an oral examination and giving the name of the defendant's local court pursuant to CCR Ord 25, r 2.

When the proceedings have been transferred, the new court shall give notice of the transfer to the judgment creditor and the debtor.

Once this has been overcome (if necessary), the application for an oral examination should be made to the court in which the debtor resides or carries on business by utilising Form N316 and payment of the fee, currently £40.00.

In a county court, the application must certify the money remaining due under the judgment and the court will issue the oral examination within five and 10 working days after receiving the form and fee.

For the first hearing, the court can send the notice by first class post to the debtor or the judgment creditor himself can agree to serve the order which should be effected a reasonable time before the day appointed for the examination. The order is in Form N37 (Order for Oral Examination of Judgment Debtor) or Form N38 (Order for Oral Examination of Another Person). There is no obligation to pay conduct money (given as defined in Chapter 1) at this stage.

If the debtor fails to appear at the oral examination, which is not unusual, an order in Form N39 will be issued at the creditor's request requiring the debtor's attendance at an adjourned hearing.

The adjourned hearing documentation (Form N39) must be served personally by either the court Bailiff or the creditor, not less than 10 days before the adjourned hearing and conduct money may have to be paid here if the debtor makes a request to the creditor not less than seven days before the hearing. A certificate must be filed by the creditor not more than four days before the hearing, certifying whether conduct money has been requested and, if so, paid.

The adjourned hearing is listed before a Circuit Judge. There have been some very recent changes in the position due to the Human Rights legislation coming into force. In essence, if the debtor does not attend the N39 hearing, then a committal order (or even a suspended committal order) will only be made if the claimant is legally represented. If the claimant is not represented, then the application will be dismissed. As the oral examination procedure takes place in the debtor's home court (which may well not be the home court of the claimant), then clearly the claimant is being put to extra expense here. If the debtor attends, the oral examination is conducted as originally intended. As this procedure could vary with local practice, it is always advisable to check the position with the local court.

7.2.3 Judgment against a Limited company

It is possible to utilise the oral examination procedure of a Director of the Limited company against whom a judgment has been obtained. A similar procedure is followed, but again the hearing must take place in the court where the director is carrying out his or her business or the court where he resides. Do not forget that this may not necessarily be the same court as that of the registered officer of the company.

7.3   Scope and nature of the examination

The debtor is required to give full and frank disclosure of his assets and liabilities (to include overseas assets), but the questions must be limited to the asset and liability position. It cannot be used as a 'fishing expedition' for further information in respect of other actions which may be taking place between the parties.

7.4   Action following the oral examination

It is vital that immediate action is taken after the oral examination pursuant to the information supplied. If property owned by the debtor is revealed for the first time and it is clear that equity exists, then proceed by way of a charging order (see Chapter 9). If details of a bank account are revealed which would appear to be in credit, then proceed by way of garnishee proceedings (see Chapter 10).

Alternatively, it may be that this procedure itself promotes an offer from the defendant to pay by instalments or even to pay in full. If this is the case, then it is hoped that the solicitor will have anticipated this and taken instructions on what sum will be acceptable to his client and can either agree to the making of the instalment order at the time or, alternatively, not accept that and seek to obtain a higher order or proceed to alternative methods of enforcement.

It is of course only a county court that has power to order judgment to be entered for payment by instalments. It is not unusual, however, for a High Court judgment to be paid by instalments, because of a private arrangement between creditor and debtor or, alternatively for there to be an order on suspension of writ of *fieri facias* for payment by instalments. The difference is that no High Court Judge can sign a judgment for instalment payments. This fundamental difference should be remembered, both generally and in relation to oral examination instalment offers.

8 Execution Against Goods

8.1 General information

Execution against goods is the most commonly used method of enforcement in debt matters. In general terms, it is execution by the seizing and sale of goods and chattels of the debtor. The procedure is undertaken by utilising a writ of *fieri facias* in the High Court (RSC Ords 45, 46 and 47) or by a warrant of execution in the county court (CCR Ord 26). Although the most common method of enforcement, it is not necessarily the most effective.

It is too easy, particularly in the county court, simply to instruct the Court Bailiff to attend to seize goods without giving detailed thought to the actual situation that exists.

A county court Bailiff will handle more warrants of execution per day than a High Court Sheriff. Although the Review Body on Civil Justice (Cmnd 394, which was the catalyst for the Courts and Legal Services Act 1990) indicated that a recovery rate for both Bailiffs and Sheriffs was broadly the same, most practitioners would question this, believing that using the Sheriff is a more effective means of recovering money than using the county court Bailiff.

Over 600,000 warrants were sent to the county court Bailiffs for issue and 47,000 warrants to the Sheriffs in the most recently published statistics, which shows a greater difference than that originally reported on in 1986.

With these caveats, then, it is advisable to ensure that the creditor knows exactly the procedure that is being adopted and the risks that exist (especially with regard to third parties laying claim to the goods) before execution is attempted.

This chapter will therefore consider the procedure to be adopted both in the High Court and county courts and the problems that arise with this form of enforcement. As has been seen earlier (in Chapter 6), since 1 July 1991, pursuant to Art 8(1) of the High Court and County Courts Jurisdiction Order 1991 SI 1991/724, enforcement by execution against goods for a sum of £5,000.00 or more may only take place in the High Court (unless the judgment is for a sum under an agreement regulated by the Consumer Credit Act 1974).

8.2   Execution against goods in the High Court – writ of *fieri facias* (RSC Ords 45–47)

8.2.1 Introduction

This is a form of execution through the Sheriff that is adopted for High Court judgments and indeed county court judgments that are transferred to the High Court for enforcement (see Chapter 6). As has been seen, the maximum figure for county court execution against goods is £5,000.00, but any judgment in excess of £600.00 can be transferred to the High Court for enforcement with all the advantages that have been discussed earlier. By this procedure, the Sheriff is authorised to attend and seize goods in his bailiwick to the value of the debt and interest and costs (including his costs) and sell the same at an auction. He undertakes this procedure through his Officer.

In the county court, the fee for issue of the warrant of execution is currently £25.00 (if the sum to be recovered is not more than £125.00) and £45.00 (where the sum to be recovered is more than £125.00). The only costs that are to be awarded to the solicitor as fixed costs is the sum of £2.25. If it is necessary to re-issue the warrant, a further fee of £20.00 is payable. All fees and costs can be added to the judgment debt and are recoverable. In the event of non-recovery, therefore, the maximum costs figure is £67.25.

In the High Court, the Sheriff's charges used to be based on the hourly rates of the Sheriff's Officers. These charges were recoverable from a debtor but, in the event of non-recovery, could be quite expensive for the creditor from whom they would then claim. This procedure has now changed and utilising the Sheriff can be a much more cost effective procedure, particularly since the commencement of the Sheriff's Lodgement Centre in 1999.

8.2.2 Sheriff's Lodgement Centre

The setting up of this particular centre is a major step forward for debt recovery practitioners.

The Centre can be contacted at 2 Sarjeant's Inn, Fleet Street, London EC4Y 1NX, telephone: (020) 7353 3640, fax: (020) 7583 2996 and the website can be found at **www.sheriff.co.uk**.

Effectively, this particular centre takes much of the administration away from solicitors and creditors and does the necessary work to issue the writ of *fieri facias* and send that to the appropriate Sheriff.

Obviously, there are costs involved, but it is recommended for ease of administration that the Sheriff's Lodgement Centre is utilised.

For this reason, detailed notes of the practice and procedure for issuing and preparing writs of *fieri facias* are not set out in this book, but rather the procedure through utilisation of the Sheriff's Lodgement Centre is considered.

8.2.3 Practice and procedure

The Sheriff's Lodgement Centre will deal with both county court judgments over £600.00 or High Court judgments. It will also deal with the transfer process for transferring a county court judgment up to the High Court for enforcement (as described in Chapter 6).

If a creditor wishes to utilise the services of the Sheriff's Lodgement Centre to transfer up his county court judgment, then he pays a fee to the Sheriff's Lodgement Centre of £29.45, which is to cover the transfer fee of £20.00, £7.10 administration fee and £2.35 lodgement fee.

The Sheriff's Lodgement Centre will then undertake all the necessary administration and aims to convert the judgment to a Sheriff's Warrant within seven to 10 days. The sealed writ of *fieri facias* is then sent to the local Under Sheriff for the seizure process to commence.

It may be the case that the creditor himself has already undertaken the transfer of process and if so, the Sheriff's Lodgement Centre will still produce the writ of *fieri facias*, arrange for it to be issued and instruct the local Under Sheriff (again for a fee of £29.45).

For High Court judgments, then, the Centre will again undertake the paperwork for the production and issue of the writ of *fieri facias* and again send it to the local Under Sheriff (again for the same price of

£29.45) and this will apply whether or not the High Court judgment is to be issued out of London or a District Registry.

Finally, if the creditor or his solicitor has prepared and completed his own writ of *fieri facias*, then the only fee payable for the checking and sending of this to the local Under Sheriff is £2.35.

In essence, what the Sheriff's Lodgement Centre is seeking to do is to take the administrative pressure off the creditor or his solicitor and, to that extent, the procedure is to be welcomed.

More importantly than the preparation, though, is the fact that the Sheriffs now offer a fixed fee to creditors if they are unable to recover monies due under the warrant.

It should not be forgotten of course that the creditor or his solicitor may have certain information concerning the debtor which will be of use to the Sheriff's Officer and, therefore, he may still wish to liaise with him and supply that information in letter form. For example, it is of little use directing the Sheriff to a registered office address of a company where there will be no assets on which to levy. This again shows the value of a pre-action questionnaire and close liaison between a solicitor and his client.

8.2.4 Levying execution

Armed with the writ and (hopefully) relevant information from the creditor's solicitor, the Sheriff's Officer will attempt to levy execution by attending at the debtor's premises. He will then either seize the goods or, and this is more common, take what is called 'walking possession' of them. This is an agreement whereby in consideration of the Sheriff's Officer not seizing the goods or leaving a man in close possession of them, the debtor agrees not to remove or otherwise deal with the goods. A short time is then allowed by the Sheriff for the debtor to find the relevant sums of money, or alternatively to reach an agreement with the creditor to prevent the goods being taken subsequently or being sold at auction. If the debtor does dispose of the goods in contravention of the agreement, he will be guilty of an offence for which he can be prosecuted.

8.2.5 Costs

Fixed costs of £71.75 are generally allowed on issuing execution, but no costs are allowed in the case of a writ of *fieri facias* unless the judgment is for £600.00 or more, or the claimant has been awarded costs (RSC Ord 47, r 4 – but this will of course very rarely apply in practice).

The creditor's solicitors should in particular note that as soon as the Sheriff's Officer attends, costs are being incurred by them and, therefore, if the debtor seeks to come to an arrangement with the creditor, it is vital that all the Sheriff's costs and expenses are ascertained and taken into account in settlement. If this is not taken into account, the creditor or his solicitor may find himself liable for those charges. In addition, as this is a High Court judgment enforcement method, interest is ongoing on the debt and costs (at the rate of 8% from the date of the certificate of judgment) and this must be calculated and added to the outstanding sum for the completion of the execution.

On a successful levy, Sheriff's costs and those of his Officer are calculated on a percentage basis of the value of the goods seized and sold. These costs called Sheriff's poundage are 5% on the first £100.00 and 2¹/₂% thereafter (see Sheriff's Fees (Amendment) Order 1982 SI 1982/89 for full details of Sheriff's fees). These charges are recoverable from the debtor.

Previously to the setting up of the Sheriff's Lodgement Centre, if a levy was unsuccessful (for any one of a variety of reasons, for example, the bankruptcy of the individual, the priority of other writs or the disappearance of the debtor), the creditor would still have to pay the Sheriff and his Officer and clear warnings had to be given to the client about this. As with any enforcement process, no guarantee of success can be given.

However, under the new system, if the Sheriff cannot levy execution, he will send an account to meet the cost of attempting to levy and this is fixed at £50.00 plus VAT. If the Sheriff is asked to re-attend or to attend a second address, then he can send a further account for £50.00 plus VAT. In addition, it should be remembered that £29.45 will normally also have been spent to commence the process.

As with any system, if a particular instruction requires further work, then charges would be agreed between the Sheriff and the creditor or his solicitor.

The initial indications are that the Sheriff's Lodgement Centre is working successfully and positively from the point of view of creditors.

8.3   Execution against goods in the county court – a warrant of execution (CCR Ord 26)

8.3.1   Introduction

A warrant of execution is the county court equivalent to the writ of *fieri facias*. It is executed by the county court Bailiff who is a salaried employee of the court. All county court Bailiffs are drastically overworked and hence the speed of response and warrants of execution can be extremely slow and, unfortunately, the success rate can also be comparatively low. There can be nothing more frustrating for a client than having paid the fee for issue of warrant of execution for him to be told that either the defendant no longer resides at the address given or there are no goods left upon which successful levy can be made. However, the warrant of execution is still the most commonly used method of enforcement in the county courts, as the figures set out earlier indicate.

8.3.2   Practice and procedure

Execution against goods in the county court must be read now subject to the overriding jurisdictional limit of £5,000.00. Any greater sum must be executed through the Sheriff, as has already been stated (unless it is a Consumer Credit Act Agreement). Normally, leave is not required unless special circumstances exist as set out in CCR Ord 26, r 5. The special circumstances mirror the High Court requirements for leave to proceed. The creditor or his solicitor completes a form of request for the warrant (Form N323). In recent years, county court forms have changed regularly and care should be taken to ensure that the correct and most up to date form is used for each method of enforcement. In addition, the appropriate fee must be paid which consists of £25.00 where the sum to be recovered is not more than £125.00 and £45.00 where the sum to be recovered is more than £125.00. To issue a warrant for recovery of land or property (Possession Warrant) is £80.00 (see Chapter 17). On Form N323 (form of request for warrant), the creditor or his solicitor must certify the amount remaining due under the judgment and, where the judgment is payable by instalments, he must further certify that the whole or part of any instalment due remains unpaid as well as the amount for which the warrant is to be issued (CCR Ord 26, r 1).

It is vital that the court is informed of any payments that are received direct after the request has been sent to the court.

It is important to remember that the application should be made to the court where the judgment was entered, or if the claim has been transferred since judgment, to that court.

Upon receipt of the warrant, the court will issue it and forward it to the Bailiff in whose area the warrant is to be executed. There is space on the request form for the claimant or his solicitor to supply details which may assist the Bailiff in respect of the execution. If this space is insufficient, a separate letter should be written.

The execution then proceeds as per the High Court execution, with the Bailiff reporting the results to the creditor's solicitor or creditor direct. Unlike the High Court, there is no Sheriff's poundage payable and once the fee has been paid to the court for the issue that is the final fee (except a further £20.00 fee is payable if the warrant is to be re-issued). However, as has been stressed before, no interest is running on the judgment, as county court judgment interest only commences at the £5,000.00 figure. These, therefore, are some of the factors to weigh up when considering a High Court or county court action. As has been said earlier, however, the removal of Sheriff's poundage in respect of an unsuccessful execution and its replacement by a fixed fee further increases the advantages of utilising the Sheriff. Further, it is sometimes thought that the Bailiff is overly conservative in his dealings with a debtor. The normal practice is for the debtor to receive a letter from the Bailiff indicating that a warrant has been issued and requesting payment. It is only if payment does not follow within a seven day period that the Bailiff will attempt to seize goods. It is not unusual at this first visit for the debtor to seek to suspend the warrant (see 8.5.10).

8.3.3 Instalment order (CCR Ord 26, r 1(2))

Where a court has made an order for a payment of a sum of money by instalments (as is quite normal in the county court) and default has been made in payment of such an instalment, a warrant of execution may be issued for the whole of the said sum of money and costs then remaining unpaid, or for part of the money due, provided that the sum is not less than £50.00 or the amount of one monthly instalment, or four weekly instalments, whichever is the greater.

In order to take advantage of this procedure which could be useful to 'test the water' against a recalcitrant debtor, the whole or part of an instalment which has already become due must remain unpaid and any warrant previously issued for part of the said sum of money and costs must have expired or have been set aside or abandoned (CCR Ord 26, r 1(3)).

In addition, reference should be made to CCR Ord 26, r 1(4). Under the previous Rule, the District Judge could direct that notice of issue of warrant was given to the debtor but, under this rule, the Court Officer must send a notice unless otherwise directed. The notice is a warning notice to the debtor that the warrant has been issued and that it shall not be levied until seven days thereafter. This means that a debtor has a normal seven day breathing space before the bailiff attends and this is another factor that should be borne in mind by those seeking to enforce.

8.3.4 County court banking process

Since 1 April 1990, there have been significant reductions in the county court banking functions. However, the county court will still handle payments under live warrants. Because the court will no longer have a record of payments, though, it will not be able to check that a defendant is in arrears when a request to issue or re-issue enforcement is received. This is of course particularly relevant for the issue or re-issue of a warrant of execution. Hence, Form N323 throws the onus onto the claimant to complete monetary details. Similarly, if a warrant of execution is to be re-issued, Form N445 is utilised and again the claimant has to certify the outstanding balance. Finally, it should be remembered that payments under a suspended warrant or payments of a part-warrant, or after the bailiff has made an abortive return are made direct to the claimant.

8.4   Writ of delivery and warrant of delivery (RSC Ord 45, r 4 and CCR Ord 26, r 16)

Brief reference to these two enforcement procedures need only be made. They are similar to the writ of *fieri facias* and warrant of execution and relate to the enforcement of a judgment for the delivery or recovery of any goods, for example, goods pursuant to Consumer Credit Act cases, although the remedies laid down by the Consumer Credit Act 1974 and the Hire Purchase Act 1965 still remain.

The High Court follows a procedure similar to a writ of *fieri facias* and in the county court, although a different form is utilised (N324 – request for warrant of delivery) the procedure is still very much akin to the issue of a warrant of execution.

8.5 Particular practical problems with an execution against goods

8.5.1 Execution against farmers

It is important to remember that the Sheriff for a High Court writ and the District Judge for a warrant of execution may well require an Agricultural Credits Act search to be produced to reveal whether any charge has been registered against the debtor farmer. To prevent delays, it may be advisable to undertake such a search at the Land Registry in any event.

8.5.2 Costs of execution

Although county court costs are generally less than High Court costs, it should be borne in mind that the only solicitors' costs allowed on the issue of a warrant of execution for more than £25.00 are £2.25, which hardly equates to costs of undertaking that issue process.

8.5.3 Goods exempt from seizure

Changes were brought about by s 15 of the Courts and Legal Services Act 1990. This section amends both s 138 of the Supreme Court Act 1981 and s 89 of the County Courts Act 1984 and widens goods which are exempt from seizure.

The most important exemptions are now:
- such tools, books, vehicles and other items of equipment as are necessary to that person for use personally by him in his employment, business or vocation (there are no monetary limits);
- such clothing, bedding, furniture, household equipment and provisions as are necessary for satisfying the basic domestic needs of that person and his family (there are no monetary limits);
- any money, banknotes, bills of exchange, promissory notes, bonds, specialities or securities for money belonging to that person.

8.5.4 Disputes as to ownership

One of the most common problems when a Sheriff or Bailiff attends is for the debtor to claim that particular goods belong to a third party and are therefore not available for execution. Obviously, if hire purchase or leasing documentation is presented and checked by the Sheriff's Officer or Bailiff, the matter can be clarified there and then, but it is often the case that ownership is claimed by the debtor's wife or another relative. There is a set procedure if a claim by a third party is made to goods seized. Notice is passed to the creditor or his solicitor and formal interpleader proceedings may well follow.

Once a formal claim is made, then the creditor has seven days for a High Court writ or four days for a county court warrant to admit or dispute the claim of the third party. This is a short time limit in which to take instructions and again indicates the need for the solicitor and his client to have worked closely together to be aware of the possible claims that may be made.

If the claim is not admitted within the time period set out, then an interpleader summons will be issued to resolve the issue as to ownership.

The procedure for interpleader proceedings is set out in RSC Ord 17 and CCR Ord 33, but it should be borne in mind that it can be expensive and time consuming. The legal costs involved may well be those not only of the solicitor's client, but also those of the third party and indeed those of the Sheriff, in the High Court.

As both writs of *fieri facias* and warrants of execution are valid in the first instance for 12 months beginning with the date of issue, if the interpleader process is ongoing for a considerable period of time, care should be taken to ensure that the execution process is renewed to protect the creditor in priority to other subsequent execution creditors.

8.5.5 Insolvency

One further common problem in execution is that the process is part underway when either the company goes into liquidation or the individual is adjudged bankrupt and the judgment creditor may well find himself thereafter dealing with the insolvency practitioner appointed to deal with the insolvency. The position is that a judgment creditor may only retain the benefit of his execution if that execution has been completed before the commencement of an insolvency process and reference should be made to the relevant sections of the Insolvency Act 1986 (ss 183, 184 and 346). An execution is completed for a writ of *fieri facias* and warrant of execution when the goods and chattels that have been seized have been sold. In addition, where the amount of the execution exceeds £500.00 and goods are sold or money paid to avoid a sale, then the monies must be retained by the Sheriff or the proper officer of the county court for a 14 day period and if notice of insolvency is received during that period, the monies must be paid to the insolvency practitioner appointed. Again, therefore, caution must be exercised with a client if execution is canvassed as an enforcement method and an individual or company is considered to be in financial difficulties.

It may be, however, that the execution route is chosen deliberately by an execution creditor to obtain a return, indicating there are no goods upon which to levy, which in itself will then enable the creditor to pursue bankruptcy or insolvency remedies (see Chapter 13).

8.5.6 Competing creditors

It is often the case that when an execution process is commenced, it is discovered that other creditors are seeking to pursue a similar remedy. In this regard, it is important to be clear upon the rules for competing writs or warrants of execution as there could be both High Court and county court ones in existence.

The basic rules are:

- in the High Court, priority is governed by the time the writ is received by the Under Sheriff for execution;

- in the county court, priority is governed by the time the request for issue is delivered to the court.

If, therefore, writs are issued both out of the High Court and warrants of execution issued from a county court, consideration must be made of the time of the delivery of the writ to the Under Sheriff or the time at which the warrant is received by the District Judge.

8.5.7 Jurisdiction

Pursuant to s 103 of the County Courts Act 1984 (as amended by s 125(2) of the Courts and Legal Services Act 1990, Sched 17, para 16 and the Civil Procedure Act 1997, Sched 2, para 2(2)), where a warrant of execution has been issued from a county court against the goods of any person, and the goods are out of the jurisdiction of that court, it should be sent to the District Judge of any other county court within the jurisdiction of which the goods are, or are believed to be, with a warrant endorsed on it, or annexed to it, requiring execution of the original warrant.

8.5.8 Restoring priority

If a writ or warrant is issued and then a judgment upon which it is based is later set aside but then restored on appeal, that writ or warrant returns to its original priority (*Bankers Trust Co v Galadari and Another* [1986] 3 All ER 794).

8.5.9 Other writs or warrants

Where a situation arises when it is discovered that other writs or warrants are in existence, before continuing with the process, consider whether or not an alternative enforcement method will be more beneficial. Bear in mind, in particular, that if bankruptcy or liquidation is commenced, this may have the effect of depriving other creditors of the benefits of their execution, but by the same token, bankruptcy or liquidation will be more expensive and there is no guarantee that it would promote the payment that is desired (see Chapter 13).

8.5.10 Withdrawal or suspension of execution process

It is not unusual of course for the commencement of the execution process to result in attempts by the debtor to come to arrangements with the creditor for either payment by instalments or for other arrangements to be made. In the High Court, if instalments payments are offered by the debtor, then the creditor should think very carefully about his future actions, because if he instructs the Sheriff to withdraw, then other creditors may be able to obtain priority by levying execution.

In addition, the Sheriff's Officer will be able to submit his claim for poundage referred to earlier. The walking possession agreement to which reference has been made could therefore remain whilst appropriate arrangements are being made, but bear in mind that Sheriff's costs will increase and any arrangement with the debtor will have to include these.

It is far more common for there to be applications for suspension undertaken in the county court by the debtor. Thus, do not be surprised if the issue of the warrant produces an application (completed by the debtor on Form N245) to suspend the warrant. Notification will be given of the terms of the suspension applied for and a decision must be taken as to how to proceed. The creditor will be sent Form N246A and as a creditor has a choice of:

• agreeing to the warrant being suspended and accepting the defendant's offer of payment;

- agreeing to the suspension but requesting that the defendant pays more than has been offered;
- refusing to agree to the warrant being suspended.

If there is a dispute as to the amount the defendant should pay, then this will initially be considered by a Court Officer, who will make a decision. If the creditor does not agree with this, then the matter will be considered at an appointment fixed before the District Judge.

If the creditor disagrees absolutely with the suspension of the warrant, then an appointment is fixed by the court when both parties can attend and the District Judge will make a decision on whether or not to allow the suspension. For the procedure under the suspension of a judgment or the execution process reference should be made to CCR Ord 25, r 8.

8.5.11 Powers of a Sheriff or Bailiff

Both Sheriff and Bailiffs can only enter a private house if they are allowed in. Entry cannot be forced. This position is different for commercial properties, in that they can break into these (providing there is no living accommodation attached and it is believed that debtor's goods are inside). If, however, these steps are taken, then the Sheriff or Bailiff will almost invariably be requesting assistance and it may be the case that the creditor is asked to give an indemnity in case the debtor makes claims against the Sheriff or Bailiff.

If unusual situations occur, then close liaison should take place between all parties involved in the process.

9 Charging Orders

9.1 Background information

A charging order can be a very effective remedy for the enforcement of a judgment and is normally taken against land or an interest in land. However, there is nothing to prevent a charging order being obtained against securities, such as shares, or funds that are in court. For the purposes of this Practice Note, however, the emphasis is on the charging order which is obtained over land. It is important to remember that the obtaining of the charge in itself will not immediately obtain the money which is the subject of the judgment. To obtain that money, there must either be an application to enforce the sale of the property, or alternatively, a voluntary sale and, providing there is enough free equity, the judgment will then be satisfied. The effect of the charging order itself is to give the creditor security for the debt.

Both the High Court and county court have powers to make charging orders over land or an interest in land and the basic procedure is set out in RSC Ord 50 and CCR Ord 31, as scheduled in the Civil Procedure Rules and in the Charging Orders Act 1979 (as amended).

It is fundamental when considering this area to be clear that a charge, be it over land or other security, creates an equitable charge for the judgment creditor over that security.

9.2 Jurisdiction

With enforcement of a judgment by way of a charging order, the county court has exclusive jurisdiction for a judgment or order of £5,000.00 or less (County Court Jurisdiction Order 1981 SI 1981/1123). To this extent, the jurisdiction given by the Charging Orders Act 1979 is not affected by the Courts and Legal Services Act 1990. Indeed, even if the amount is over £5,000.00, then the county court has concurrent jurisdiction with the High Court.

As has been mentioned previously (in Chapter 6), a county court judgment for a sum greater than £600.00 can be transferred to the High Court for enforcement by way of a writ of *fieri facias*. But in respect of enforcement by way of a charging order, this procedure can only be undertaken where the judgment sum is greater than £5,000.00.

The court does not have any jurisdiction to make a charging order when payments under an instalment order in the county court are not in arrears (*Mercantile Credit Co Ltd v Ellis* (1987) *The Times,* 1 April).

One interesting variation in the county court procedure is that, pursuant to CCR Ord 31, r 1(1), it is possible to apply for a charging order either in the county court in which the judgment was obtained or to the court for the district in which the debtor resides or carries on business, which would of course normally be the county court for the district in which the property is situated.

9.3   Enforcement by charging orders in the High Court (RSC Ord 50)

9.3.1 Procedure

In fact, the procedure to be adopted for both High and county court charging order applications is relatively similar. There are always two stages to any charging order application:

- the without notice application for the charging order *nisi*; and
- the hearing for the charging order absolute of which the debtor is given notice.

The requirement for the charging order *nisi* in the High Court is a without notice application by witness statement or affidavit to the Practice Master or District Judge as the case may be.

A fee of £50.00 is payable (for each person against whom your order is sought) (see Chapter 17) pursuant to Supreme Court Fees Order 1999 (SI 1999/687, as amended by SI 2000/641). A witness statement or affidavit should depose to the following:

- Details of the judgment and the amount unpaid at the date of the application.

- The name and address of the judgment debtor and of any creditor of his whom the applicant can identify.
- Full identification of the asset which is to be charged.
- Proof by the person making the statement or the deponent (which will be the solicitor or creditor) that the asset which is the subject of the application is owned beneficially by the judgment debtor, with details of the reason for that belief and the witness statement or affidavit must exhibit any documentary evidence to support the same.

As to belief of beneficial ownership, the creditor may be able to supply evidence from a Land Charges search or from the Land Registry or alternatively there may be letters from the debtor himself or an oral examination confirming the position. Alternatively, a prior mortgagee may have confirmed the position. Each case must be judged on its own merits.

Previously for registered land, there was a request in the affidavit for an order for the Land Registry to supply office copies of the entries on the Register pursuant to s 112 of the Land Registration Act 1925 (as amended). The Land Registration Act 1988 has replaced this section and there is now a provision which gives a right to inspect the Register and the documents referred to therein. This applies as from 3 December 1990 pursuant to SI 1990/1359. Creditors and their solicitors should therefore avail themselves of the open Register provisions.

Upon considering this evidence, it is hoped that the order is made and indeed a draft order should be submitted to the court with enough copies for service. The form of order to utilise is Form No 75, found in the Practice Direction supplementing CPR Part 4 (Table 2). If a charging order is sought on stock or shares in more than one company, then a separate order must be drawn up in respect of each company. It will then be for the judgment creditor to serve the debtor with the order and this should be done together with the witness statement or affidavit which was sworn to obtain the order.

The order will have a specified return date for the hearing of the application for a charging order absolute and the debtor would then have to attend to show cause why the order should not be made absolute. RSC Ord 50, r 2(1) also sets out other persons to be served in certain more specialised situations.

Immediately after obtaining the charging order *nisi*, it is incumbent on the creditor to register the charge before service (see 9.6.1).

Unless the court directs otherwise, the order must be served by the judgment creditor by post or personally to comply with CPR 6.2 at least seven days before the return day. Service is effected on the judgment debtor and on any other known creditors of the judgment debtor and any other interested persons.

Thus, it is always advisable to ensure that a witness statement or affidavit of service is available at the hearing of the charging order absolute to prevent any point being taken by the District Judge that the order has not been served. The solicitor should also attend at the hearing of the charging order absolute with a draft order as the responsibility is on the creditor to draw up and serve that order. Vital time will be saved if this is all prepared beforehand.

The form of order is set out in Practice Form No 76 from the Practice Direction supplementing CPR Part 4 (Table 2). As this is a High Court judgment, interest is running at the normal judgment interest rate (currently 8%).

Where a charging order is sought and made absolute, basics costs of £160.00 are added to the debt together with additional costs of £18.00 if an affidavit of service is required (see Chapter 17), and together with such reasonable disbursements in respect of search fees and registration as the order of the court may allow.

9.4   County court enforcement of charging orders (CCR Ord 31)

9.4.1 Procedure

The procedure is very similar to that utilised in the High Court and set out in CCR Ord 31. Again, the procedure is undertaken initially by a without notice application by witness statement or affidavit with the details as set out in CCR Ord 31, r 1(2) being included (these are similar to the High Court requirements).

In addition, as would often be the case, where it is a High Court judgment, there must also be lodged (see CCR Ord 25, r 11):

- an office copy of the judgment;
- if a Writ of Execution has been issued – a copy of the Sheriff's return;
- further, the affidavit (or witness statement) should verify the amount unpaid at the date of the application.

There are also fees of £50.00 to be paid (see Chapter 17).

Upon receipt of the documentation, the court will then place the matter before the District Judge and if, as is hoped, the order is made, that order will be drawn by the court (to save time, the judgment creditor may wish to draw the order). This will be as prescribed Form N86 (see Table 3 in the Practice Direction supplementing CPR Part 4). The courts no longer serve the order, but it is for the judgment creditor to serve it in accordance with CPR Part 6 and to ensure that an affidavit of service or witness statement of service is lodged at court before the charging order absolute hearing. Service must be effected not less than seven days before the day fixed for the further consideration of the matter (CCR Ord 31, r 1(8)).

At the further hearing, the District Judge has a discretion either to make the order absolute, with or without modifications, or discharge it (CCR Ord 31, r 2) and he has a duty to consider not only the parties to the application, but also other creditors as far as they are known. It is for this reason that the witness statement or affidavit sworn on the without notice application has to disclose the names of other creditors who may be affected by the application. Further copies of the charging order *nisi* and the witness statement or affidavit are to be served on these creditors so named unless the District Judge directs otherwise (CCR Ord 31, r 1(6)).

Particular problems associated with the position of other creditors are considered in 9.6.2 and 9.6.3.

If the court makes the order absolute then it will be in Form N87 (Table 3 in the Practice Direction supplementing CPR Part 4). It will then be served by the court on the same persons as the order *nisi*.

9.4.2 Costs

Fixed costs of £71.00 are allowed on the charging order absolute in the county court. If it is a High Court judgment being enforced in the county court, interest still runs on the judgment debt, notwithstanding the making of the order in the county court (*Board of Trade v Okapo* [1989] 5 CL 328). In addition, the court and oath fees are allowed as disbursements provided a schedule is given to the court signed as correct. It used to be that disbursement would not be allowed as a matter of course. This is not now the case, but some District Judges will disallow oath fees on the grounds that witness statements could be used instead or affidavits could be sworn at the county court free of charge.

9.5   Orders for sale following a charging order and the appointment of a receiver

9.5.1 Background

It may be that the judgment creditor is content to sit back and rely on the security that the charging order (duly registered) affords. Alternatively, it may be known that a sale of the property is in progress and as, inevitably, a purchaser's solicitor will require the charge to be removed prior to purchasing, an appropriate undertaking from the debtor's solicitor to discharge the debt upon the sale may be sufficient. As with any solicitor's undertaking, ensure that it is carefully and properly worded to protect the creditor client.

However, in the absence of either a pending sale or a satisfaction by other means, the creditor may wish to enforce his charging order, either by a sale or by the appointment of a receiver.

9.5.2 Enforcement of a charging order by sale (RSC Ord 88 and CCR Ord 31, r 4)

In the High Court, the procedure is by a claim form in the Chancery Division (even if the judgment was obtained, as is normally the case, in the Queen's Bench Division). The procedure is set out in RSC Ord 88, r 5A.

In the county court, proceedings are commenced by a claim form together with a witness statement or affidavit. The details of the witness statement or affidavit contents are set out in CCR Ord 31, r 4(1).

One practical problem with an order for sale, which has exercised the courts, has been where a charging order is held over one person's beneficial interest in co-owned land only (for example, against one or two joint owners, who normally are husband and wife). Under previous law, an order for sale could be obtained pursuant to an application under s 30 of the Law of Property Act 1925 (see *Midland Bank plc v Pike* [1988] 2 All ER 434). Now, such a creditor can make an application under s 14 of the Land and Appointment of Trustees Act 1996.

9.5.3 The appointment of a Receiver (RSC Ords 30 and 51)

It is appropriate to consider this matter in this chapter although it is a procedure that is rarely exercised. Reference is also made to this remedy in Chapter 12 (12.2). It is not limited, however, to the appointment pursuant to a charging order, but in all cases in which it appears to the court to be just and convenient to appoint a receiver.

Given that other methods of protection are available, this power should need to be exercised on relatively few occasions. In particular, possibly, where there is fear that in the absence of protection some property may be dissipated. In this case, the procedure can be used swiftly and an interim receiver appointed.

The court will ensure that the receiver has the necessary powers to obtain money for the creditor from the assets specified in the order.

In the High Court, an application notice is taken out before the Master or District Judge, with a witness statement or affidavit in support which will have to depose to the reasons why the order is being sought (Ord 51). The relevant forms are the forms for the appointment of a receiver (Form No 82) and the order appointing the receiver (Form No 84) both in the Practice Direction supplementing CPR Part 4.

In the county court, under the old regime, the procedure was governed by CCR Ord 32, but this is not a scheduled rule and therefore RSC Ord 30 regulates both High Court and county court procedure.

If consideration of the appointment of a receiver is to be made to protect the proceeds of sale of land, then the costs of such an application must be considered and discussed with the creditor. A receiver is normally a solicitor or accountant and he will often not take office unless satisfied that the assets will be adequate to meet his remuneration , or alternatively that he has been given a complete indemnity by the judgment creditor. As other professional persons become involved, the costs increase proportionately.

As stated above, do not only consider the appointment of a receiver in respect of the protection of proceeds of sale of land, but a receiver could also protect an interest that the debtor has in, for example, income from a trust fund.

9.6 Practical problems concerning charging orders

9.6.1 Registration

As stated above, an equitable charge created by a charging order needs to be protected by registration; this should be undertaken at both the charging order *nisi* and the charging order absolute stages.

A different procedure should be adopted depending on whether the charge relates to:

- unregistered land; or
- registered land.

(a) *Unregistered Land*: A charging order is protected by registration at HM Land Registry of a writ or order affecting land pursuant to s 6 of the Land Charges Act 1972. Form K4 is used and the cost is £1 per name registered.

If this is done and the land is subsequently disposed of, any person purchasing the land will be bound by the charging order unless he is able to take free from it through the priority period given by an official search certificate. Indeed, if there is fear that the land will be disposed of prior to the registration of the charging order, it is possible to apply for the registration of a pending action at the land registry. Form K3 is used and the cost is £1 per name registered.

Considerable problems have been caused when considering the registration of a beneficial interest rather than the legal estate itself. This situation could, of course, arise when the judgment is against one joint owner. In the case of *Perry v Phoenix Assurance plc* [1988] 1 WLR 940, it was stated that a charging order for an interest under a trust for sale (rather than a legal estate) cannot be registered as a writ or order. Statutory registrations are sometimes accepted by the Land Charges Registry, but technically are of no protection to the creditor. His remedy would be to pursue an order for sale pursuant to s 30 of the Law of Property Act 1925 (see *Midland Bank plc v Pike* [1988] 2 All ER 434).

In addition, in this circumstance, the other owner or owners should be notified of the charge and this notification may be sufficient protection for the creditor. All prior mortgagees and other chargees should also be notified.

(b) *Registered Land*: If the charge is against the whole legal estate, then this is registered by way of a notice on the charges register. This is undertaken by completing Form AP1, HM Land Registry for which a fee of £40.00 is payable.

If the charge relates solely to an interest under a trust for sale, registration is by way of a caution against dealings. There is a risk that the caution registration could be 'warned off' on the grounds that it does not relate to land and by analogy to *Perry v Phoenix Assurance plc*. The registration of a caution is undertaken by completing form CT2 HM Land Registry and the fee is £40.00.

As can be seen, therefore, a charging order against the interest of one joint owner of property is no guarantee to successful enforcement. In practice, however, nearly all purchasers of properties so charged would seek undertakings from the vendor's solicitor (that is, the debtor's solicitor) that the charges were removed and it is hoped therefore that normally the problems that technically exist would be overcome.

9.6.2 The discretion of the court

The granting of a charging order absolute is within the discretion of the court and it must consider not only the interests of the debtor and creditor but other creditors. Other persons interested in the application should be disclosed in the witness statement or affidavit and copies of the charging order *nisi* and a witness statement or affidavit is served on them. Interested parties could be other creditors affected by the proposed charge or possibly another joint owner, for example, in a matrimonial situation, the other spouse.

If it is known that matrimonial difficulties exist, then a judgment creditor could well be faced with an application by the spouse to intervene in the proceedings.

A number of cases have considered the priority of a spouse's claim in matrimonial proceedings as against a charging order absolute and the results are conflicting (which only serves to highlight the discretion that is vested in the court). For a statement of the principles, see *Harman v Glencross* [1986] 2 WLR 637 and *Austin-Fell v Austin-Fell* [1990] 3 WLR 33.

Frequently, a debtor faced with a charge over his property will apply for a varied order to pay by instalments. Many courts use this discretion given to allow that varied order and dismiss the charge.

9.6.3 Insolvency

A common difficulty arises when a charging order *nisi* has been obtained and before the hearing of the charging order absolute the debtor becomes insolvent either by being made bankrupt or, in the case of a company, being wound up. The judgment creditor is clearly concerned as to whether he can retain the benefit of his charging order or whether it will be overturned at the charging order absolute hearing. The relevant law is set out in ss 183 and 346 of the Insolvency Act 1986 which deal with the definition of 'completion of execution'.

The leading authority is *Roberts Petroleum v Kenney (Bernard)* [1983] 2 AC 192, which sets out the general principles to be applied in such a situation. The House of Lords held that if a debtor was adjudged bankrupt, or in the case of a company wound up, after the making of a charging order nisi, then this may be sufficient on its own to prevent the order being made absolute as it would be prejudicing creditors generally.

If, however, a judgment creditor is able to hold security successfully against an insolvency practitioner subsequently appointed in the bankruptcy liquidation, he should liaise carefully with him as to what he proposes to do in relation to the property because the insolvency practitioner himself has powers of sale prescribed by the Insolvency Act 1986.

9.7   Conclusion

It is only worth undertaking a charging order application if a creditor is satisfied that not only does the debtor have an interest in the property to be charged, but also that there are no prior charges which remove the equity. There will be nothing more frustrating than to advise a creditor that he is protected by a charging order only to find that, once the building society or bank has been paid, the amount of equity that is passed on is insufficient to satisfy the creditor. However, sometimes there are no other assets available and invariably property prices go up rather than down so a charge may offer security for the future. Having obtained a charge, there is nothing to stop the creditor taking other methods of enforcement.

10 Garnishee Proceedings

10.1 Background information

The relevant rules are to be found in RSC Ord 49 and CCR Ord 30, both of which are scheduled in Sched 1 and Sched 2 respectively to the CPR.

The basis of this enforcement procedure is that if the debtor himself is owed money, then these monies can themselves be attached by the judgment creditor in order to obtain his money.

The basic procedure in both the High and county court is the same and the minimum judgment sum in respect of a garnishee order which may be made in both courts is £50.00.

The most common situation is where the creditor is aware that the debtor's bank account is in credit and an application is therefore made to garnishee that bank account. This includes not only current, but also deposit accounts and would also cover building societies and other like institutions.

It must be remembered, however, that no order can be made to reduce below £1.00 the amount standing in the name of the judgment debtor in a building society or credit union account (RSC Ord 49, r 1(4) and CCR Ord 30, r 1(5)).

Examples of other debts that can be attached are as follows:
- a debt due under a dishonoured or stopped cheque;
- future instalments of a debt payable by instalments;
- monies in the hands of the sheriff under an execution (providing that money is to be paid to an individual and not to the court);
- most salaries when due as a debt (subject to certain exceptions).

The following have been held to be debts not attachable:

- dividends distributable amongst creditors in the hands of an official receiver;
- salary accruing but not due;
- unliquidated damages, amounts not yet ascertained;
- fees due from a solicitor to counsel.

These are not exhaustive pursuant to RSC Ord 49 and CCR Ord 30.

In both the High Court and county court, application is made without notice by filing a witness statement or an affidavit.

10.2 Practice and procedure in the High Court (RSC Ord 49)

10.2.1 Garnishee order *nisi* and absolute

As with the charging order procedure, there are two stages, namely the garnishee order *nisi* and absolute.

The *nisi* is obtained without notice and the witness statement or affidavit must set out the following information:

- The name and last known address of the judgment debtor.
- The judgment or order to be enforced and the amount of such judgment or order and the amount remaining unpaid at the time of the application.
- State or depose that, to the best of the information or belief of the witness or deponent, the garnishee (giving name, address and details) is indebted to the judgment debtor, and state the source of this information or belief.
- Where the garnishee is a deposit taking institution having more than one place of business, give the name and address of the branch at which the judgment debtor's account is believed to be held and the number of that account, or (if it be the case) state that all or part of the information is unknown to the witness or deponent. Also give the Head Office address of the garnishee. The witness statement or affidavit should be as set out in Practice Form PF 100 (as listed in Table 2 in the Practice Direction supporting CPR Part 4).

When dealing with a deposit taking institution having more than one place of business, it is therefore good practice to serve the order not only at the Head Office, but also at the branch office, or, if the exact branch office is unknown, at all those at which it is considered the account could be.

Ensure that when lodging the witness statement or affidavit, a draft order is also lodged with enough copies for service and when the order is made by the Master or District Judge, a return date will be entered. Service should then be effected on both the debtor and the garnishee.

The relevant form of garnishee order *nisi* is Practice Form No 72 from the same Table in the Practice Direction supplementing CPR Part 4.

The fee for applying for a garnishee order in the High Court is £50.00 in respect of each party against whom the order is sought (see Chapter 17). Of course, the important person to serve is the garnishee and he must be served at least 15 days before the hearing and should be served personally. If the affidavit or witness statement includes an application for permission to serve by post, then that may be done though it should be remembered an order giving this permission will need to be drawn and served. An appropriate affidavit or witness statement as to service should be prepared in readiness for the fact that the garnishee may not attend the further listed hearing.

As to the debtor, there is no requirement to serve personally. Service must be at least seven days before the appointment and seven days after the order has been served on the garnishee. The debtor's non-attendance at the hearing of the garnishee order absolute will not be fatal.

For obvious reasons, the garnishee should be served first to prevent the debtor seeking to deal with any money prior to the garnishee having notice of the same.

If these requirements are complied with, then this matter will proceed to the garnishee absolute hearing where the garnishee could attend and seek to prevent the order being made. It is often the case that correspondence has taken place between the creditor and the garnishee prior to the hearing of the order absolute. The judgment creditor's solicitor should attend at the hearing with the order prepared (Practice Forms Nos 73 and 74 in Table 2 supporting the Practice Direction at CPR Part 4 depending on whether the garnishee owes more or less than the judgment debt) and if the order is made it is then served on the garnishee.

10.2.2 Costs (see, also, Chapter 17)

Under RSC Ord 49, the garnishee is able to deduct for his costs (before payment to the applicant) the sum of £23.00. The judgment creditor's costs are calculated as follows:

- if the amount recovered is less than £150.00 – one half of the amount recovered;
- if the sum recovered is not less than £150.00 – £148.50;
- where the garnishee fails to attend the hearing and an affidavit of service is required – an additional £18.00.

All figures are taken from RSC Ord 62.

10.3 Practice and procedure in the county court (CCR Ord 30)

10.3.1 Garnishee order *nisi* and absolute

The procedure as set out in Ord 30 is in essence the same as set out for the High Court above. CCR Ord 30, r 2 details the information that must be supplied in the affidavit or witness statement which mirrors that of the High Court. The suggested form is Form N349 in the county court (Table 3 in the Practice Directions supplementing CPR Part 4). In particular, it should be noted that the witness statement or affidavit must certify the amount of money remaining due under the judgment and that the whole or part of any instalment due remains unpaid (CCR Ord 30, r 2(e)).

As with normal county court procedure, the order would be drawn up by the court (although to save time, it may be that the creditor would wish to lodge the draft order for the garnishee order *nisi*). There is a set fee payable of £50.00 to issue this application (see Chapter 17).

The prescribed form of order for the garnishee order *nisi* is Form N84. For the garnishee order absolute, the relevant form is N85 (Table 3, Practice Direction supplementing CPR Part 4).

It is submitted that the best procedure would be for the creditor to serve the garnishee to ensure that proper service is effected as it is imperative for garnishee proceedings to be effective for service to take place when it is believed money will be available. The 15 day period before the hearing applies, as in the High Court, and the debtor is served (postal service is allowed) at least seven days after the garnishee and at least seven days before the return day (CCR Ord 30, r 3).

The order will of course have the return day set out thereon and at that hearing, the garnishee can attend and the court will consider whether or not the order should be made absolute or otherwise. If there is a major dispute, then the hearing of the garnishee order absolute will in essence be a directions hearing and the determination of the dispute will take place at a later date.

There has been a major change in the garnishee procedure from 1 April 1990. Previously, the garnishee could pay into court the sum due to the debtor (or a smaller sum if that covered the judgment debt) and that would stay proceedings. This procedure has now been changed to bring the county court practice into line with the High Court. The garnishee is required to freeze any money at the *nisi* stage and, if so ordered, to pay that to the claimant at the absolute hearing. This is in line, of course, with the general curtailment of the county court banking functions. The change revoked CCR Ord 30, r 4 and is effected by SI 1989/1838, r 43.

10.3.2 Costs (see Chapter 17)

If the judgment creditor recovers less than £70.00, then he is allowed to recover in costs half the amount recovered. Where not less than £70.00 is recovered, costs of £46.50 are is allowed. (CCR Ord 38, r 18).

10.4 Practical problems

10.4.1 The court's discretion

In both the High and county court (RSC Ord 49, r 4 and CCR Ord 30, r 7), confirmation is given that the court does have a discretion in deciding whether to make absolute a garnishee order *nisi*.

The court must consider not only the judgment creditor, the judgment debtor and the garnishee, but also the position of other creditors of the judgment debtor (see *Rainbow v Moorgate Properties Ltd* [1975] 2 All ER 821).

The garnishee order is in essence an equitable remedy and it will not generally be granted if the effect is to prefer one creditor above another, if for example there is an insolvency situation. For a full explanation of this, see *Roberts Petroleum Ltd v Bernard Kenny Ltd* [1983] 2 AC 192.

With garnishee proceedings, there is no onus to provide details of other creditors. In practice, if there is a valid judgment which is in arrears and the garnishee confirms there were monies available as at the date and time of service, the order will be made absolute. It is only where the debtor can prove that the money was to be utilised elsewhere (for example, wages that would pay the mortgage on a property) that the order may not be granted.

Bear in mind as well that if the court decides not to make the order absolute in its discretion because of a liability dispute, then the judgment creditor could be involved in lengthy proceedings which again could act to his detriment and could mean that other creditors choosing other methods of enforcement may jump ahead. This, however, is not likely to be a common occurrence and, in any event, other methods of enforcement can be applied for at the same time as the garnishee proceedings are being undertaken.

Where the garnishee fails to respond to the order *nisi* in writing and does not attend the hearing and dispute the amount, then the court may, if it thinks fit, make an order absolute. Such an order can be enforced against the garnishee in the same way as any other order.

In practice, of course, a garnishee in this position may then apply to the court to vary the order by utilising the 'overriding objective' provisions of the CPR. The outcome would depend on the discretion of the court but, it is submitted, at the very least, it should result in the garnishee having to pay the creditor's costs.

10.4.2 Particular rules for deposit taking institutions

Quite apart from a garnishee's right to deduct costs as set out earlier there are particular rules for deposit taking institutions who may deduct a further £55.00 for administrative expenses when complying with an order (the Attachment of Debt (Expenses) Order 1996 SI 1996/3098). This makes it particularly important to ensure that the figures on the order are correct as to the amount to be paid over, especially as this sum maybe deducted even if the amount attached is insufficient to cover both the deduction and the judgment debt.

10.4.3 Crown debts

These generally cannot be attached (see RSC Ord 77, r 16 and CCR Ord 42, rr 13 and 14). As for the National Savings Bank, monies deposited in that bank can be attached pursuant to s 27 of the Crown Proceedings Act 1947 (as amended), which proceedings are very similar to garnishee proceedings.

10.4.4 Insolvency

It has already been seen that in other types of enforcement, a judgment creditor could come into conflict with an insolvency practitioner. The question to be asked is whether the execution is complete. For the purposes of a garnishee order, the execution is complete when the creditor receives payment from the garnishee and this entitles him to retain the benefit of execution (s 183 of the Insolvency Act 1986).

10.4.5 Striking at the right time

A garnishee order can be an effective enforcement procedure providing the creditor is reasonably certain of the information which may have perhaps been obtained through an oral examination when bank account details or building society account details are revealed. However, there is an element of risk involved and garnishee orders notoriously cause problems, particularly in the case of bank accounts.

It is particularly important to realise that an order will only be effective if money is in the account by way of a clear credit balance at the date of service of the order. Yet again, therefore, the importance of full information being available cannot be over-emphasised.

11 Attachment of Earnings

11.1 Background information

Somewhat unusually, this particular method of enforcement is only available through the county court (with only very limited exceptions). The exceptions are:

- the High Court may make an attachment of earnings order to secure payments under a High Court maintenance order;
- the magistrates' court may make an attachment of earning order to secure payment under a magistrates' court maintenance order; the payment of a fine, costs, compensation or the payment of legal aid contribution order.

See s 1 of the Attachment of Earnings Act 1971.

Subject to the above, the county court has unlimited power and jurisdiction to deal with an attachment of earnings for any debt, providing the judgment is for a sum of not less than £50.00. However, an order may be made for a sum under £50.00 if that consists of the balance of a judgment originally of £50.00 or more (see CCR Ord 27, r 7(9)(a) and (b)).

If the solicitor or his client is aware that the debtor is in employment, then this could be an effective procedure whereby payments would be automatically deducted from the debtor's wages and paid to the court. Despite the changes in the county court's banking function from 1 April 1990, the court will still receive payments under full attachment of earnings orders and in cases of maintenance only for suspended attachment of earnings orders. It is the Centralised Attachment of Earnings Payment System (CAPS) in Northampton that is responsible for collecting payments.

It may be the case that an oral examination has already revealed employment details, enabling this procedure to be adopted. Remember, however, that there is a minimum sum below which an employee's wages are not allowed to fall (called the protected earnings rate) and therefore for employees on low wages, this procedure may not be suitable.

The relevant law is to be found in the Attachment of Earnings Act 1971 and also CCR Ord 27 (CPR Sched 2). Practitioners should note the Maintenance Enforcement Act 1991 which enables a county court making a qualifying periodical payment order also to make an attachment of earnings order. This can be undertaken at the same time as the periodical payment order is made or later and either be of the courts own motion or by separate application.

11.2 Practice and procedure in the county court (CCR Ord 27)

In order to apply for an attachment of earnings order, the claimant or his solicitor must complete and file at court:

- Form N337 (request for an attachment of earnings order) (CCR Ord 27, r 4(1)) and duly certify the amount due and owing and that the whole or part of any instalment due remains unpaid.

  (Unless otherwise stated, county court forms utilised for the attachment of earnings procedure are set out in Table 3 in the Practice Direction supplementing CPR Part 4).

- If the judgment is for £5,000.00 or more, lodge two copies of the certificate giving details of the interest (CCR Ord 25, r 5(A)).

- The fee of £50.00.

It is a wise step to search in the debtor's home court for existing attachment of earnings orders (see Chapter 2). Any person with a judgment can undertake this search. If an attachment of earnings order is found to exist, then the creditor may wish to consider consolidation with an existing order (see 11.4). There is no fee for this search.

11.2.1 Procedure for non-county court judgments

As with other methods of enforcement, there should always be lodged the certified copy judgment and the certificate or witness statement verifying the amount due, and, for a High Court judgment where a writ of *fieri facias* has been issued, a copy of the Sheriff's return (CCR Ord 25, r 11).

11.2.2 Venue (CCR Ord 27, r 3)

The appropriate county court is the one in which the debtor resides. This may of course not be the court in which proceedings had been commenced and the judgment obtained and therefore a transfer should be undertaken (CCR Ord 25, r 2). A request in writing (a letter form is sufficient) is made to the District Judge of the court in which the judgment or order was obtained stating the reasons for the appropriate transfer.

There is a safety procedure if the creditor does not know where the debtor resides, in that an application can be made to the court in which a judgment or order, sought to be enforced, was obtained (CCR Ord 27, r 3(2)).

11.2.3 Procedure prior to hearing

The court will normally serve the application (Form N55) on the debtor, together with an appropriate form of reply (Form N56). He has eight days to file a reply and a copy is then sent to the creditor.

In an attempt to streamline the procedure the court, acting through the court officer, may make an attachment of earnings order on the basis of the information received from the debtor without the attendance of either party (CCR Ord 27, r 7(1)).

If an order is made in this way it is served on the judgment creditor and debtor and either party may apply on notice for the order to be reconsidered by a District Judge but this must be done within fourteen days of service (CCR Ord 27, r 7(2)).

It should be noted that the procedure whereby applications can be disposed of without attendance of either party does not apply to attachment of earnings applications for maintenance orders.

If the court officer does not consider that he has enough information to make an order he will refer the application to the District Judge and if he considers that he is able to make the order, he will do so initially without attendance of either party (with the same provisions applying for either party to request a hearing if dissatisfied with the order made) or he may fix a date for the hearing and both parties will be given at least eight days' notice (CCR Ord 27, r 7(4), (5) and (6)).

11.2.4 Further attachment of earnings procedure

If the debtor has complied with his obligations set out above, then the order will be made based on the information made available (see 11.2.6). Regrettably, it is often the case that the debtor fails to comply with his obligations and, therefore, appropriate enforcement procedure is set out in the Attachment of Earnings Act and Rules (the basic procedure is set out in CCR Ord 27, r 7A) and, in essence, enables the court to issue orders to be served personally demanding that the debtor responds (County Court Form N61). If this procedure does not provoke a response, then a further form is served (County Court Form N63) to show cause why the debtor should not be imprisoned. Although, therefore, ultimate sanction of committal to prison exists, it is rarely exercised as the consequences of non-attendance or non-compliance do finally influence the vast majority of debtors.

If these steps result in compliance, then the matter proceeds as before with either orders being made without the attendance of either party or a hearing being fixed before the District Judge.

11.2.5 Obtaining information from the employer

By CCR Ord 27, r 6, at any stage of the proceedings, a form (N338) can be sent to any person appearing to have the debtor in his employment and this requires the employer to supply a statement of the debtor's earnings and anticipated earnings with such particulars as may be so specified.

Further, by CCR Ord 27, r 15 and s 14 of the Attachment of Earnings Act 1971, the court can order an employer to supply particulars of the debtor's earnings.

The order is in Form N61A and must be endorsed with a penal notice to a named individual of the employer ordering him or her to supply particulars of the debtor's earnings.

11.2.6 Amount of the order

There are two phrases that are always utilised in attachment of earnings applications:

- normal deduction rate (NDR);
- protected earnings rate (PER).

The NDR is the amount which should be deducted regularly (normally weekly or monthly depending on how the debtor is usually paid) by the employer from a debtor's wages.

The PER is the minimum amount that the debtor must retain from earnings and is calculated by having regard to his resources and needs.

District Judges and courts are given tables of assistance in fixing the protected earnings rate although these are not binding. Practice can vary from court to court although in the past it has been clearly accepted that no debtor should go below subsistence level as defined by Income Support.

It should be noted as well, that an employer is allowed to charge £1.00 per deduction (following the 1991 amendment to s 7(4) of the Attachment of Earnings Act 1971). For this reason, many debtors would prefer monthly rather than weekly orders.

11.2.7 Costs (CCR Ord 27, r 9) (see Chapter 17)

Costs are available for each attendance on the hearing of an application for an attachment of earnings order. The fixed costs sum is £8.50 plus court fee (CCR Ord 38, r 18 Appendix B, Part 111, para 6).

11.3 Administration of an attachment of earnings order

Obviously, if the information revealed through this procedure is that the debtor is self-employed or unemployed, no attachment of earnings order can be made and the application will be dismissed. However, if an offer is made by the debtor, then an instalment order for payment of the debt could be made, but the creditor should be given an opportunity to be heard. Similarly, a suspended attachment of earnings order could be made (see 11.5).

Subject to the above, if employment is continuing, then the monies will be deducted with reference to the protected earnings rate, and the creditor will be paid, hopefully regularly. The order obviously will lapse if there are periods of unemployment.

One common problem is a change of employment. The previous employer has an obligation to notify the court of the termination. Unfortunately, there is no positive obligation on a new employer to see whether or not an attachment of earnings order is in force. If, however, he learns of one, he must notify the court and, hopefully, the order having been redirected to him will continue as before.

The Attachment of Earnings Act 1971 does lay down offences if employers fail to carry out these requirements and indeed there is a similar obligation on a debtor to notify the court of a change in employment.

However, it has to be said that in practice the enforcement of such orders is not easy if a debtor is regularly changing employment. Under CCR Ord 27, r 16, the District Judge has power to issue a summons pursuant to offences laid down in the Attachment of Earnings Act 1971 to order the defaulter to attend and show cause why there should not be punishment.

11.4 Consolidated attachment of earnings orders

Where there is already an attachment of earnings order and other applications are received then there is power to make consolidated orders (CCR Ord 27, rr 18–22 and s 17 of the Attachment of Earnings Act 1971). The procedure is laid out in CCR Ord 27, r 19 and can be applied for by the debtor or by any creditor applying for an attachment of earnings order. It can only be made, however, with notice to all creditors. By CCR Ord 27, r 20, if there is already an attachment of earnings order in force and a subsequent application is made and there is no application for a consolidated order, the court can make one of its own motion after all persons have had an opportunity to be heard.

CCR Ord 27, r 22 indicates how the court is to deal with payments under a consolidated attachment order and they are dealt with proportionately to the amounts payable. The court does have power to declare a dividend but this is rarely undertaken.

It should be noted that if an administration order is made (see Chapter 12), then these are often supported, if the debtor is in employment, with an attachment of earnings order.

11.5 Suspended attachment of earnings orders

Through the power conferred by s 71(2) of the County Courts Act 1984, an attachment of earnings order can be suspended. If the debtor makes an offer to pay the debt by instalments, then making an order suspended on the instalment terms may be to the creditor's advantage. The debtor may well not wish his employer to know that he has this judgment and may be prepared, therefore, to agree a higher instalment order than would otherwise have been the case. The threat of the attachment of earnings order being made if the instalments are not kept to, with possible employment consequences, may be a potent one for the debtor. County Court Form N64 is utilised for a suspended attachment of earnings order. The debtor may well contact the creditor direct when completing Form N56 with a request for a suspended order, and if both parties consent, this order could be made without attendance.

11.6 Practical problems

As stated above, although, in theory, the procedure should be an effective way of obtaining regular monies, the orders are often not so successful in practice due in the main to:

- the fact that they do not apply to a self-employed or unemployed person;
- the problems caused by a debtor changing employment regularly or employment lapsing with no notification being made to the court;
- a failure of employers to co-operate with the court;
- the fact that in the main these orders are dealt with by the court who often fail to chase the debtor or employer adequately.

In addition, if the individual subsequently becomes bankrupt, then the attachment of earnings order will not be effective. The court may indeed automatically discharge it in any event.

Despite the above, if an oral examination or information from the creditor reveals that the debtor has been employed with one particular employer for a considerable period of time and the prospects seem fair for that employment to continue, then an attachment of earnings order should be an efficient way of proceeding. As the majority of orders are now dealt with without the attendance of creditors or their solicitors, the costs should be kept to a minimum even though the procedure can sometimes be somewhat slow in execution.

12 Specialised Methods of Recovery

12.1 Background information

Earlier chapters have dealt with the most common methods of enforcement of a judgment, but there are others which are available and, in particular circumstances, can be of assistance. This chapter deals with those and also deals with the particular problems of satisfying judgments against a partnership and the Crown. Chapter 13 deals with enforcement of judgment by way of insolvency which has its own practice and procedure.

The more specialised methods available are as follows:

- Equitable execution (12.2)
- Sequestration (12.3)
- Judgment Summonses (12.4)
- Administration orders (12.5)
- Execution against the debtor's person by committal (12.6).

12.2 Equitable execution

It has already been seen in 9.5.3 that after obtaining a charging order, there can follow an application for a sale or the appointment of a receiver, and the phrase 'equitable execution' covers the appointment of that receiver. Historically, it grew up, as did all equitable remedies, to cover gaps in the common law remedies and is now to be found in s 37 of the Supreme Court Act 1981 and RSC Ords 30 and 51 (as scheduled in the CPR) and s 107 of the County Courts Act 1984. RSC Ord 30 regulates the procedure both in the High Court and county court. In general terms, this procedure is not utilised regularly, but it does not only occur following a charging order as it covers the appointment of a Receiver to collect assets generally and pay any debts or expenses. Such applications often have an injunction linked to them and the procedure has now been tidied to comply with CPR Part 23.

12.3 Sequestration

This is a specialised remedy which has in the comparatively recent past attracted media attention, most commonly when sequestrators attempt to deal with assets of trade unions involved in employment disputes, or in large fraud cases.

In essence, this is a remedy when a body or person is in contempt of court by disobeying an order. It is a remedy that is solely available in the High Court and the procedure is laid down in RSC Ord 46, r 5 (CPR Sched 1).

The judgments or order that may be enforced by a writ of sequestration are:

- those that require a person 'to do an act' within a specified time which can be extended if necessary;
- those that require a person to abstain from 'doing an act'.

In both cases, permission to proceed must be obtained because of the serious nature of this remedy. This is requested of a judge by application notice in accordance with CPR Part 23 and, if granted, a writ is then issued to the sequestrators to take possession of property or chattels of the person, corporation or body which is in contempt.

As can be deduced from the above, it would only be very rarely and in large claims that this procedure would be contemplated. A detailed study of RSC Ord 46, r 5 and the case law that has developed around it should be undertaken if this procedure is to be carried out.

Some protection is afforded to third parties who may wish to claim that goods subject to the sequestration are theirs and they have an opportunity to apply to the court for an enquiry to take place.

12.4 Judgment summonses

A judgment summons however can be a very useful remedy within its field. It exists to enforce only:

- maintenance arrears;
- income and certain other specialised taxes.

The relevant law is found in CCR Ord 28 (CPR Sched 2).

12.4.1 Practice and procedure

As with most county court remedies, it is enforced in the district in which the debtor resides or carries on business (CCR Ord 28, r 1) or, if the summons is to be issued against two or more persons jointly liable under the judgment or order sought to be enforced in the court for the district in which any of the debtors reside or carries on business.

The familiar procedure is undertaken for the obtaining of this judgment summons, namely the lodging of:

- a request (Form N342 – Table 3 from the Practice Direction supplementing CPR Part 4);
- fee – £80.00 (see Chapter 17);
- the Interest Certificate in duplicate if judgment is for £5,000.00 or more (CCR Ord 25, r 5A).
- affidavit or witness statement.

The documentation must be served personally and a sum for the travelling expenses of the debtor should be tendered.

It should also be remembered that if a High Court judgment is to be enforced the normal rules for extra documentation (CCR Ord 25, r 11) apply.

The documents must be served not less than 14 days before the date fixed for the hearing (CCR Ord 28, r 3) and, as with an attachment of earnings order, if the debtor fails to appear, the threat of committal hangs over him with further process to be served.

If the debtor appears, the normal order (if it seems he can pay) would be for a committal order suspended for a further time to enable payment to be made (CCR Ord 28, r 7).

Alternatively, the court could dismiss the judgment summons or make a fresh periodical payments order or make an attachment of earnings order.

Therefore, although limited in scope, the threat of committal hanging over a debtor can be a very effective way of enforcing a judgment if the criteria are satisfied. Certainly, in matrimonial cases, it should be considered as a swift way to enforce maintenance arrears, and possibly a more effective way of proceeding than with other rather longer and more drawn out remedies.

12.5 An administration order (CCR Ord 39)

This procedure requires a debtor to pay to all his creditors who are subject to the order an amount calculated in proportion to the amount owing to them and this is to be paid by instalments. Payment can be either in full or at an agreed number of pence in the pound.

Reference has already been made to this remedy in Chapter 11 concerning attachment of earnings orders. It is only available in the county court and is one that is useful for debtors for, in effect, it enables him to schedule his creditors and pay over a period of time. Whereas, therefore, an order is clearly for the benefit of the debtor, it is not good news for a creditor, in that it will inevitably mean a long wait for payment. In essence, the debtor will supply to the court a list of all his creditors and the amounts owed and the court will then consider all the creditors together and make a decision upon the debtor's proposals for payment.

12.5.1 Practice and procedure

This is set out in CCR Ord 39 and ss 112 to 117 of the County Courts Act 1984. It was proposed that these sections were to be amended by s 13 of the Courts and Legal Services Act 1990. The most fundamental change was the abolition of the £5,000.00 limit on the judgment debt and, secondly, the procedure enabling a judgment creditor as well as a judgment debtor to apply for an order. Somewhat surprisingly, these changes have still not been brought into effect.

An administration order is made in the court of the district in which the debtor resides or carries on business (CCR Ord 39, r 2(1)).

Furthermore, they can either be on the application of the debtor, or by the court on its own motion pursuant to an oral examination (CCR Ord 39, r 2(2)) or, as has been seen, pursuant to an attachment of earnings application.

Obviously there must be in existence a county court judgment and the total amount of debts must not exceed that jurisdiction (currently £5,000.00).

If the debtor desires such an order then he lodges at court a request for an administration order in Form N92 (Table 3 in the Practice Direction supplementing CPR Part 4).

In addition, if on an application for an attachment of earnings order, the court considers that the debtor has other debts he shall be ordered, with a view to the making of an administration order, to furnish to the court a list of all his creditors and the amounts which he owes to them. This is undertaken on Form N93 in the county court.

In both cases, the statements made are verified by sworn statements (CCR Ord 39, r 3). CCR Ord 39, r 5 then lays down the procedure for the application to be considered on paper by a court officer. If there are objections to the decision of the court officer, then the papers are put before a District Judge when a hearing is fixed on 14 days' notice.

A procedure also exists for creditors to object to the inclusion of any debt within the proposed administration order. This objection must be given not less than seven days before the day of the hearing and be lodged at court, together with reasons for the objection, and the documents sent to the debtor and the creditor whose debt is being objected to (Ord 39, r 6).

12.5.2 Procedure on hearing

There are different outcomes depending on the attendance or non-attendance of the debtor:

(a) *Debtor fails to attend*: If the debtor fails to attend, then the application should either be struck out or adjourned. As has been said, the procedure is for the benefit of the debtor and it is true to say, because of the work involved, it is not popular with county courts. Therefore, it is essential that a debtor is present before any order is made. A failure by the debtor to comply after the event will also mean that the procedure is revoked.

(b) *Attendance of debtor (CCR Ord 39, r 7)*: At this hearing, creditors may be present and the District Judge will check through the schedule of debts and deal with the same and check also that any amended amounts referred to in information supplied by creditors have been correctly entered. If further debt information comes to light, then the hearing may be adjourned to give creditors an opportunity to be heard. If the District Judge is satisfied, however, that the amended list still does not exceed the county court limit of £5,000.00, he can proceed to make the order which is in Form N94. Copies will be served on:

- the debtor;
- every creditor from the list of debts;
- any other creditor who has subsequently proved his debt; and

- all courts which to the knowledge of the District Judge have a judgment against the debtor or proceedings pending for debts (see CCR Ord 39, r 9).

District judges do tend to exercise discretion wherever possible in this particular procedure. For example, if some of the debts listed are effectively joint debts between husband and wife and it is the husband applying for the administration order, then they may well halve the debt if that will assist bringing the debtor within the £5,000.00 limit.

The order is posted in the office of the court for the district in which the debtor resides.

Power does exist by s 112(6) of the County Courts Act 1984 for an order to provide for payment of the debts to such extent as appears practicable and District Judges have been given guidance to avoid orders which would proceed for a number of years. It is felt that such orders would not give any incentive to the debtor in view of the length of time that would be taken to finalise the order, and given the fact that most bankruptcies are discharged after three years.

12.5.3 Power to review the order (CCR Ord 39, r 14)

To take account of future changes in a debtor's position, there is power to review an administration order. A court which is satisfied that the debtor is unable to pay any instalment due can suspend the order, at the same time and on such terms as it thinks fit, or vary the order. Although this would appear to be an advantageous procedure for the debtor, the sanction is that if he does not comply with any terms and is found to have acted unreasonably, then the scheme can be revoked.

Alternatively, it can be converted to an attachment of earnings order as a consolidated order which would possibly give more security for the creditors whilst the debtor remains in employment.

12.5.4 The addition of later debts

In theory, there is no difficulty with the addition of later debts and indeed, even if those later debts take the total outside the county court limit, there is still the discretion in the procedure for the administration order to stand (s 112(5) of the County Courts Act 1984). However, a debtor who incurs subsequent debts may not be dealt with as sympathetically by the court.

The procedure for subsequent proof by creditor is set out in CCR Ord 39, r 11 and the normal practice of giving notice to the debtor and other creditors for them to object to the addition is provided for. If no objection is given within a seven day period after notification, the debt is added, but subsequent creditors will rank for payment of a dividend after current creditors (s 113(d) of the County Courts Act 1984).

12.5.5 Effect of an administration order

The advantage to the debtor is that no further enforcement procedure can be undertaken without leave of the court, but the sanction is that if he fails to comply with the scheme, it will be revoked.

Money is collected by the court who deduct 10% from that sum and then pay the remainder to creditors on a *pro rata* basis at six monthly intervals.

From a creditor's point of view, such orders are not very satisfactory because they are generally made against debtors who have no reasonable prospect of paying within a short period of time and , because county court judgments under £5,000.00 do not carry interest, there is no protection for the creditor for the delay in receiving payment. However, in certain cases, given the impecuniosity of the debtor, the view may be taken that some money being received is better than none at all, even over a long period of time.

12.6 Execution against the debtor's person by committal

Reference need only be briefly made to the power to commit. It has already been seen that failure to comply with certain enforcement procedures (notably the oral examination, attachment of earnings and the judgment summons) can lead to the threat and ultimately the carrying out of a committal order. Such powers are very rarely exercised and the threat is often sufficient to ensure that the required step in the enforcement proceedings is carried out. From a practical point of view, the advantage to a creditor of a committal warrant being exercised must be questioned if, as is often the case, the reason for debts being placed in the hands of a solicitor is to ensure that money is received. For the sake of completeness however, reference should be made to RSC Ord 52 and CCR Ord 29. There is a Practice Direction supplementing these orders which is RSC PD 52. Both powers are similar and include the power to commit a director or officer if the party in contempt is a company.

If this procedure is to be followed then many cases have stressed that it must be followed exactly and a failure to do so will result in the order not being made. See *Williams v Fawcett* [1996] QB 604 and *Harmsworth v Harmsworth* [1987] 3 All ER 816.

12.7 Satisfaction of orders against a partner

The advantages of issuing proceedings against individual partners rather than a firm have already been stressed. Certain enforcement procedures can follow as of right whereas leave is required in other circumstances.

12.7.1 Enforcement of judgment or order against firm as of right (RSC Ord 81, r 5 and CCR Ord 25, r 9)

A judgment or order against a firm may be enforced against:

- any property of the firm;
- any person who admitted in the action or matter that he/she was a partner or is adjudged to be a partner;
- any person who was served individually as a partner and failed to appear in the proceedings.

12.7.2 Enforcing judgment against a firm with permission of the court

In circumstances other than the above, permission of the court is required and it includes execution against a member of the firm who was out of the jurisdiction at the date of issue of the proceedings. In addition, by RSC Ord 81, r 6 and RSC Ord 25, r 10, it is not possible to issue execution to enforce a judgment between a firm and its members without permission of the court.

Although permission to proceed will often be granted by the relevant court, it is a further step in the proceedings which could be avoided if proceedings are issued against the partners personally at the outset.

However, it may be the case, of course, that the partnership itself has assets and a judgment has been obtained against one partner. In this case pursuant to RSC Ord 81, r 10 and s 23(2) of the Partnership Act 1890 (for a county court), a procedure exists for a charge to be obtained against that partner's interest in partnership property.

12.8 Satisfaction of orders against the Crown

This is a specialised subject in itself and reference should be made to RSC Ord 77 and CCR Ord 42 (as scheduled in the CPR). The law is set out in the Crown Proceedings Act 1947. There is no prohibition against bringing a default action against the Crown, but special rules exist if further information is requested by the Crown.

Further, no default judgment can be entered against the Crown except with permission of the court and no application for summary judgment against the Crown can be made.

When it comes to enforcing a judgment, none of the normal methods are available and instead a certificate of judgment is obtained which is then served on the solicitor for the Crown (this applies for the service of all documents in Crown proceedings).

Because of the specialised nature of these proceedings, if a solicitor is instructed to pursue a Crown body, there is no substitute for analysing the relevant High Court and county court rules and ensuring that the client knows of the peculiar nature of this procedure.

It is of course comparatively rare that this procedure is necessary in general debt work.

Pursuant to s 17 of the Crown Proceedings Act 1947, the Minister for the Civil Services publishes a list of Authorised Government Departments and the Names and Addresses for Service of the person who is, or is acting for the purposes of the Act as, solicitor for such Departments. From a practical point of view, assistance may be gained from the Treasury Solicitor's Department, Queen Anne Chambers, 28 Broadway, Westminster, London SW1H 9JX. Their telephone number is (020) 7210 3000.

13 Insolvency

13.1 Introduction and sources of law

The Insolvency Act 1986 revolutionised the law relating to both personal and corporate insolvency and the use of insolvency proceedings in debt recovery is now well established. However, the courts have been quite clear that insolvency remedies should not be utilised as debt collecting tools except as a last resort. This also makes practical sense, for it must be remembered that if insolvency proceedings are commenced, then the creditor could find that he will only be recovering a small proportion of his debt (for quite an expensive outlay!). The basic difference between the use of insolvency as a debt collection tool and more conventional debt recovery methods is that the creditor in a bankruptcy or liquidation situation will have to share any monies recovered with other creditors. Hence, it may well be the case that only a small proportion of the debt is recovered.

However, the threat of bankruptcy or liquidation may well produce payment in full and a solicitor should always consider this particular remedy with his client.

There are also other advantages to be considered, namely:

- the appointment of a liquidator or a trustee in bankruptcy could enable other routes to be explored for the benefit of creditors. For example, the activities of the directors in a company can be investigated, possibly to the financial advantage of the creditors (see 13.5);

- previously, the automatic availability of VAT bad debt relief in an insolvency situation as opposed to other debt recovery situations was considered to be an advantage. This has been eroded somewhat over the years by changes in the VAT bad debt relief scheme which is now much more widely available on bad debts generally than before. For details of the scope of the current scheme, reference should be made to any local office of HM Customs & Excise.

13.1.1 Sources of law

The basic law is found in the Insolvency Act 1986, which is divided into separate parts and those relevant to this Practice Note are:

* Part IV, which deals with the winding-up of companies;
* Part IX, which deals with the bankruptcy of individuals.

In addition there are a number of statutory instruments that have been issued pursuant to the Insolvency Act 1986, the most important being:

* Insolvency Rules 1986 SI 1986/1925. There have been a number of Insolvency (Amendment) Rules issued following these original Rules in 1987, 1989, 1993 and 1995.
* The Insolvent Partnerships Order 1986 SI 1986/2142 and the Insolvent Partnerships Order 1994 SI 1994/2421.
* Insolvent Companies (Disqualification of Unfit Directors) Proceedings Rules 1987 SI 1987/2023.

There exists a special procedure for dealing with insolvent partnerships. Partnerships may be wound up as unlimited companies under Part V of the Insolvency Act 1986 and the individual partners may be made bankrupt under Part IX of the Insolvency Act 1986.

There have been two subsequent Insolvency Acts (Insolvency Act 1994 and Insolvency (No 2) Act 1994) but these are not relevant for the purposes of this text.

Fundamentally, however, a new Insolvency Act 2000 received the Royal Assent on 30 November 2000. At the time of writing, no date has been fixed for the coming into force of the relevant provisions, but it does make some fundamental changes to insolvency law, particularly in the area of rescue procedure.

Inevitably, with the coming into force of the Civil Procedure Rules, it was necessary to bring out amendment rules in insolvency law to bring this area into line and reference should be made to the Insolvency (Amendment) Rules 1999 SI 1999/359 and the Insolvency (Amendment) (No 2) Rules 1999 SI 1999/1022.

Finally, although reference will not be made in any detail to it in this book, the Company Directors Disqualification Act 1986 is the legislation which enables courts to disqualify those who have been directors of companies which have become insolvent, from taking directorships subsequently.

Practice Directions (PD) and Practice Notes (PN) are regularly published in this area of law and care should be taken to keep up to date with the publishing of such directions. These normally form amendments to the procedure to be followed pursuant to the Insolvency Act 1986 and any subsequent legislation and deal with developing areas of law.

13.2 The statutory demand

13.2.1 Introduction

The statutory demand is one of the methods by which a bankruptcy or liquidation is triggered and it is not even necessary for there to be a judgment of the court for this procedure to be utilised.

A number of forms have been prepared for insolvency work and these are readily available from law stationers. The forms are prescribed by the Insolvency Rules 1986 SI 1986/1925 and set out as Sched 4 to these Rules. For the purposes of the statutory demand, the following forms should be utilised:

- Form 4.1 for the winding-up of a company.
- Form 6.1 for a liquidated sum payable immediately by an individual.
- Form 6.2 for a liquidated sum payable immediately by an individual following a judgment or order of the court.
- Form 6.3 for a debt payable by an individual at a future date.

It is absolutely vital that the correct forms are used and that they are filled in correctly.

Particular points to note are as follows:

- State the debtor and creditor and relevant address.
- Set out full details of the money due, how the debt has arisen and whether any interest has been claimed.
- Ensure the form is signed by an individual (if solicitors are drafting this document, then the individual solicitor should sign rather than his firm).
- For bankruptcy cases, state the court to which application should be made to set aside the statutory demand, which is the county court for the insolvency district in which the debtor resided or carried on business for the last six months. In this regard, it is important to remember that not all county courts have bankruptcy jurisdiction and reference should be made to the index of county courts which

can be found in civil procedure text to make sure this section is completed correctly.

13.2.2 The statutory demand and the individual debtor

To issue a statutory demand against an individual, there must be a debt which is equal to or exceeds £750.00 (or, alternatively, an aggregate amount of debts to this level).

Besides stating the appropriate court for applying to set aside the document (see 13.2.1 above) the document must also state that, if there is to be an application to set aside, then action must be taken within 18 days from the date of service.

Service of a statutory demand on an individual is, except for exceptional circumstances, to be effected personally. The exceptions are, in general terms: if the debtor is deliberately avoiding service, in which case, there is the option of postal service; insertion through a letter box; advertising in a newspaper; or applying to the court for an order for substituted service.

It is important to realise however that a District Judge or Bankruptcy Registrar will be loath to make a bankruptcy order unless he is absolutely certain that all proceedings including the statutory demand have come to the attention of the debtor.

13.2.3 The statutory demand and the corporate debtor

Pursuant to s 123(1)(a) of the Insolvency Act 1986, if a creditor to whom a company owes more than £750.00 then due has served on the company at its registered office a statutory demand in the prescribed form requiring the company to pay the sum due and the company has for three weeks thereafter neglected to pay the sum or to secure or compound for it to the creditors' reasonable satisfaction, then that company is deemed unable to pay its debts and the creditor is able to petition for its winding-up.

Although there are conflicting authorities on the point, best practice (to avoid later disputes) is to ensure that the statutory demand is personally served at the registered office of the company. Unlike the individual debtor, there is no court specified to which application should be made to set aside the statutory demand (and consequently no 18 day period). If the debtor does dispute the document, then the appropriate course will be to apply to the court for an injunction restraining the presentation of a winding-up petition.

13.2.4 Case law concerning statutory demands

There has been much case law surrounding the statutory demand and its proper use as a debt collecting tool. The thrust of present cases is that if there is any indication to a creditor that there is a dispute over the debt, then it is quite wrong to try to prevent the debtor from pursuing that dispute by the service of a statutory demand.

One of the earlier cases was *Re A Company (No 12209 of 1991)* [1992] 1 WLR 351, which was a case concerning a company debt. Mr Justice Hoffman found that the debt was clearly disputed and stated that the use of statutory demand was an abuse of process and he struck it out and (importantly for practitioners) ordered costs against the creditor on an indemnity basis.

This position was taken further in the case of *Re A Company (No 006798 of 1995)* [1996] 1 WLR 491. In this case, a winding-up petition was issued without a statutory demand and based simply on non-payment of a debt. Here, Mr Justice Chadwick made a wasted costs order against the petitioner's solicitors on the grounds that a solicitor who deposed in an affidavit in support of a winding-up petition that the company was insolvent, acted improperly if he did not have that belief and he acted unreasonably if there were no grounds upon which a competent solicitor could reach that view on the material available to him.

Clearly, therefore, solicitors must be very careful when advising clients upon the utilisation of insolvency proceedings and these should only be used when there is a clear undisputed debt.

Conversely, however, a failure to complete the statutory demand forms fully and correctly will not necessarily invalidate the statutory demand – see *Re A Debtor (No 1 of 1987)* [1989] 2 All ER 46. The test to be applied is whether or not the debtor has been misled or suffered injustice. If he has not, and even if the form has not been filled out correctly in every detail the proceedings should still be allowed to continue.

It is only in the case of a statutory demand served upon an individual that an application can be made to set it aside. In the case of a statutory demand served on a company, if the debt is disputed or there are other reasons to dispute the statutory demand, then the debtor company will have to apply for an injunction to restrain the presentation of a winding-up petition.

Upon the hearing of an application to set aside the statutory demand against an individual in accordance with the Insolvency Rules, the

District Judges have tended to apply the test of considering whether the debtor is able to show a 'triable issue'. If he can, the creditor will certainly find that the statutory demand is set aside and he will have to embark on conventional debt recovery proceedings. The circumstances in which the court may set aside a statutory demand are contained in paragraphs (a) to (b) of r 6.5(4) of the Insolvency Rules 1986 and reference should be made to those.

13.3 Individual bankruptcy

13.3.1 Grounds for petitioning for bankruptcy

Apart from the statutory demand ground (which has been set out in 13.2.2), a creditor can present a bankruptcy petition against an individual if £750.00 or more is due and owing and execution or other process issued in respect of the debt on a judgment or order of the court has been returned unsatisfied in whole or in part. The normal situation therefore is that a writ of *fieri facias* has been returned without levy by the Sheriff's Officer, or a warrant of execution has been similarly returned by the county court bailiff. However, if it is the case that the Sheriff or Bailiff has not been able to meet with the debtor and effect a levy, then the courts have said that in these circumstances there is no proof of insolvency and a statutory demand should first be served if bankruptcy is to be utilised.

Obviously, for the obtaining of a bankruptcy order pursuant to the failure of execution, a judgment or order must have been obtained, but this is not necessary if a petition has been based upon a statutory demand. It is sometimes the case that a statutory demand is served to test the response from the debtor before conventional debt proceedings are issued.

13.3.2 Practice and procedure

Prescribed forms in the Insolvency Rules 1986 (Sched 4) exist and for an individual these are as follows:

- Form 6.7: failure to comply with the statutory demand for a liquidated sum payable immediately.
- Form 6.8: failure to comply with a statutory demand for a liquidated sum payable at a future date.
- Form 6.9: execution on a judgment has been returned in whole or in part.

- Form 6.10: on default in connection with an individual voluntary arrangement (as defined in Part VIII of the Insolvency Act 1986).

The original petition, together with one copy for service and one to be exhibited pursuant to the affidavit or witness statement of service and a further one for the petitioning creditors' file, is prepared. The original petition is exhibited pursuant to an affidavit or witness statement which verifies the facts of the petition (Form 6.13, Insolvency Rules 1986, Sched 4). In addition, where the petition is based on a statutory demand, an affidavit or witness statement of service exhibiting that statutory demand must be filed at court.

A deposit of £350.00 for the Official Receiver's fees is paid to the court, together with the issue fee which is currently £150.00 (see Chapter 17). It is important that the petition document is completed correctly and issued in the correct court (which will be the insolvency district where the debtor has resided or carried on business for the greater part of the six months immediately preceding the presentation of the petition). This will normally mean that proceedings are issued in the county court, although if a debtor has resided or carried on business within the London insolvency district then the High Court has jurisdiction.

A search should be done in the county court or the High Court to see if a bankruptcy petition has been issued by another creditor. If this is discovered, then, obviously, a further petition should not be issued, but contact made with the petitioning creditor's solicitors indicating that support will be given and if that creditor is paid then the petition should be taken on by the further creditor.

Unlike company winding-up petitions, bankruptcy petitions are not advertised.

13.3.3 The bankruptcy hearing

Bankruptcy hearings take place before a District Judge or Bankruptcy Registrar in chambers and it is always advisable to attend with a draft order (in triplicate). In addition, the District Judge or Bankruptcy Registrar must be informed of any notification received from other creditors, who either wish to support or oppose the petition.

There are a variety of orders which can be made on the hearing of the petition. In general terms, these are:

- the adjournment of the petition;
- the dismissal of the petition;
- substitution of another creditor in place of the petitioning creditor;
- the withdrawal of the petition;
- the actual making of a bankruptcy order.

If a bankruptcy order is made, then the official receiver is immediately informed and he will act, until a trustee in bankruptcy (who must be a licensed insolvency practitioner) is appointed.

The costs orders that can be made depend upon the outcome of the hearing, but if a bankruptcy order is made, then the normal order would be for the petitioning creditor's costs to be assessed if not agreed and to be paid from the estate itself.

13.4 The corporate debtor

13.4.1 Grounds for liquidation

As this Practice Note is concerned with actions of creditors, this section is concerned solely with a compulsory winding-up order. It should be remembered, however, that a company can place itself into voluntary liquidation, or alternatively, may find itself struck off the register at Companies House for failure to deal with statutory requirements. Before embarking, therefore, on any winding-up proceedings, an up to date company search should be obtained, not only to see whether other creditors have taken proceedings, but also to see whether other insolvency processes have taken place.

These may include the appointment of an administrative receiver by an individual or institution (normally a bank) which holds a debenture or charge over the company's assets. The appointment of an administrative receiver does not prevent winding-up proceedings following, but it is a strong indication of the unlikelihood of assets being available to satisfy the debt.

The statutory demand as a ground for winding-up a company has been set out in 13.2.3. Apart from that, the following grounds exist to trigger the issue of a winding-up petition for a compulsory liquidation:

- the company is unable to pay its debts;
- the court is of the opinion that it is just and equitable that the company should be wound-up;

- the company has by special resolution resolved that it be wound-up by the court;
- in addition, there are certain technical grounds where a winding-up petition would not be commenced by a creditor, but by the company itself.

For the purpose of a creditor, the most important ground is that the company is unable to pay its debts as and when they fall due.

The most common grounds are the statutory demand ground or the failure of a writ of execution. Remember that for the statutory demand, the debt must be greater than £750.00. This limit is not, however, necessary to commence proceedings through unsatisfied execution.

13.4.2 Practice and procedure

The prescribed form of the petition is Form 4.2 (Insolvency Rules 1986, Sched 4) and the original petition must be exhibited pursuant to the affidavit or witness statement verifying the petition, which is set out in prescribed Form 4.3 (Insolvency Rules 1986, Sched 4). In addition, a copy for service should be taken to the court, with a further copy to be exhibited pursuant to the affidavit or witness statement of service. It is always sensible to have one additional copy to retain on the solicitor's file.

A deposit of £500.00 for the official receiver's fees must be paid, together with a fee of £150.00 to the court. The official receiver's deposit, as with individual bankruptcy, will be refunded if the petition is dismissed or withdrawn.

A winding-up petition can be commenced in either the High Court or (if the paid up share capital is £120,000.00 or less) in the county court which has jurisdiction for the area where the registered office is situated. Not all county courts, however, have winding-up jurisdiction and therefore reference should be made to the county court index in the relevant civil procedure texts.

The petition itself must be served in accordance with Insolvency Rule 4.8, which provides that it should be served at the registered office in any of the following ways:

- handed to a person who acknowledges himself to be (or to the best of the server's knowledge, information and belief is) a director or other officer, or employee of the company; or

- it may be handed to a person who there and then acknowledges himself to be authorised to accept service on the company's behalf; or
- if no person is there, as set out above, it may be deposited at or about the registered office in such a way that it is likely to come to the notice of a person attending at the office.

There are also provisions, if service at the registered office is not practicable, to serve it at the company's last known principal place of business, or by delivering it to the secretary or some director, manager or principal officer.

Personal service should be effected, although there are provisions as to substituted service if this is required.

A winding-up order is advertised in the *London Gazette* (prescribed Form 4.6, Insolvency Rules 1986, Sched 4), which must take place at least seven business days after service and at least seven business days before the hearing.

A certificate of compliance (Form 4.7, Insolvency Rules 1986, Sched 4) must be lodged at court at least five days before the hearing of the petition.

13.4.3 The compulsory liquidation hearing

This is heard by the District Judge or Bankruptcy Registrar in open court. Other creditors may support and if appropriate be substituted as the petitioning creditor. The petitioner must prepare for the court a list of the names and addresses of all those who had notified him of their intention to appear and hand that list to the court on the day of the hearing.

At the hearing, the court may:

- make a winding-up order;
- dismiss a petition;
- adjourn the hearing conditionally or unconditionally;
- make an interim order;
- make any other order it thinks fit.

If negotiations are continuing, then the petition may well be adjourned although the courts have indicated that these should only be for short periods.

Costs are at the discretion of the court, but if the order is made for winding-up, they will be paid out of the estate.

The official receiver is immediately informed once a winding-up order is made and he will then administer the estate pending the calling of a meeting and the appointment of a liquidator who will be an insolvency practitioner.

13.5 Procedure after the insolvency

The official receiver who will act initially in both bankruptcies and liquidations will, in most cases, call a meeting of creditors and at that meeting, a trustee in bankruptcy or liquidator will be appointed. If the creditor is not able to attend the meeting, there are provisions for proxy votes to be submitted. As a matter of practice, however, creditors should be encouraged to attend meetings to ensure their views are known.

Once the insolvency practitioner is appointed as trustee in bankruptcy or liquidator, then he will investigate the affairs of the individual or company and the Insolvency Act 1986 gives him a number of powers to look at transactions which have taken place and, in certain circumstances, he may be able to recover funds for the benefit of creditors.

For a detailed analysis of his powers, reference should be made to the Cavendish Practice Note on *Insolvency Law* by Steven Frieze.

13.6 Other insolvency proceedings

Although outside the scope of this practice note, the Insolvency Act 1986 created a set of insolvency procedures which in general terms were attempts to provide rescue operations for individuals or companies in financial trouble. The latest Insolvency Act 2000 (to be brought into force on a date to be fixed) further amends certain of these procedures. These are:

- an individual voluntary arrangement (Part VIII of the Insolvency Act 1986);
- a company administration order (Part II of the Insolvency Act 1986);
- receivership (Part III of the Insolvency Act 1986);
- company voluntary arrangements (Part I of the Insolvency Act 1986);

In addition, under the Deeds of Arrangements Act 1914, deeds of arrangement still exist for individuals, but these are rare.

If a creditor is notified of any of these specialised insolvency procedures, then legal advice should immediately be taken as to the consequences for monies that are owed.

14 Injunctions and Their Use in Debt Recovery

14.1 Background information

There is often a fear amongst creditors that the debtor will seek to hide or move assets in such a way as to make a judgment unenforceable. The law recognises this problem and, accordingly, a series of remedies has been developed to help reduce this problem and to assist in debt recovery.

In the vast majority of debt actions, these remedies will not be necessary, but if there is a genuine fear then they are there to be used. Such remedies are often called 'pre-emptive' because, as injunctions, they can be undertaken without notice to the other party.

The three particular pre-emptive remedies which are most commonly seen in debt recovery work are:

- freezing injunctions (domestic and worldwide) (formerly known as Mareva injunctions);
- search orders (formerly known as Anton Piller orders);
- writ *ne exeat regno*.

The first two remedies are found in CPR Part 25 and the Practice Direction supporting this, which Part is headed 'Interim Remedies' and it should be studied in detail if these procedures are to be invoked. Reference also should be made to the most up to date editions of the relevant parts of the Commercial Court Guide and the Chancery Guide.

The third remedy is much more specialised and will be considered briefly at the end of this chapter.

14.2 Freezing injunctions

CPR 25.1(i)(f) confirms that the court may grant as an interim remedy an order restraining a party from removing from the jurisdiction assets located there or restraining a party from dealing with any assets whether located within the jurisdiction or not.

The essence of this procedure is that the court can grant either before or after judgment an injunction against the debtor on a with or without notice basis if it is satisfied that there is the risk that the debtor's assets will either be removed from the jurisdiction of the court (that is, from England and Wales) or be otherwise dissipated, even if they are not located within this jurisdiction.

In addition by CPR 25.1(i)(g), the court may grant as an interim remedy an order directing a party to provide information about the location of relevant property or assets or to provide information about relevant property or assets which are or maybe the subject of an application for a freezing injunction.

This particular remedy has been continually developing and was given statutory authority by s 37(3) of the Supreme Court Act 1981.

The County Court Remedies Regulations 1991 SI 1991/1222 (as amended by the County Court Remedies (Amendment) Regulations 1995 SI 1995/206) removed the general power of the county court to grant freezing injunctions subject to certain limited exceptions as set out in reg 3. Furthermore, it may be the case in county court proceedings, either actual or contemplated, that such an injunction is required. In this situation, an application can be made to the High Court and then the proceedings re-transferred to the county court (see regs 4 and 5 of the County Courts Remedies Regulations 1991(as amended)).

When the procedure was originally developed, it was really concerned with cases where there was some foreign element (for example, where the defendant had links with another country), but that requirement is no longer absolutely necessary.

However, because the nature of this remedy is often to proceed without notice to the other party, the court must be satisfied that full disclosure is made by the applicant of all the relevant facts, so that it can judge the matter fairly.

14.2.1 Procedure

Application for a freezing injunction will be made by application notice following the provisions of CPR Part 23 which sets out the general rules concerning applications for court orders. In addition, any applicant must follow the Practice Direction (interim injunctions) which supplements CPR Part 25.

The important points to note as set out in that Practice Direction are as follows:

- The normal application is to a High Court Judge although, in certain cases, Masters and District Judges have the power to grant injunctions.
- The application notice which seeks the order must be supported by affidavit evidence.
- The application notice and evidence in support must be served as soon as practicable after issue and not less than three days before the court is due to hear the application.
- A draft order should be filed at the same time.
- It is possible to make applications for a freezing injunction where a claim form has not yet been issued and also to make such applications without notice to the respondent.
- In cases of extreme urgency, a telephone hearing can take place and the court can accept an undertaking from the applicant's solicitor to issue the claim form immediately.
- Applications outside normal working hours can be dealt with in accordance with the procedure laid down in the practice direction supporting CPR Part 25.

Probably the most important document is the affidavit and the requirement of full disclosure is enforced strongly by the courts who have regularly recognised the Draconian nature of the remedy. In *Brinks-Mat Ltd v Elcombe* [1988] 1 WLR 1350, the court stated that the duty of the applicant was to make a full and fair disclosure of all the material facts. This is an objective test and the court will require proper inquiries to be made before the application is lodged.

Each case will depend on its own facts, but if proper enquiries have not been made because of time constraints, the court should be told of this.

Clearly the most important paragraph of the affidavit supporting the application is the reasoning for the belief that assets will disappear and it is the duty of the applicant to set out all material facts of which the court should be made aware. If the application is made without notice, then an explanation as to why this procedure has been followed must also be included.

If an order is granted, then (unless the court otherwise orders) the applicant must give an undertaking to the court that if the court finds that the order has caused loss to the respondent, and that the respondent should be compensated for such loss, the applicant will comply with any order for damages in favour of the respondent which the court may make. In certain circumstances, this could be quite a severe undertaking and no person should consider it lightly. The court may also ask the applicant to give an undertaking to give a written guarantee from a bank to support the damages undertaking.

If the procedure has been successfully completed, then the order is served personally. Because the order takes effect as soon as it is given, service of not only the order, but also the other documents in support must be undertaken forthwith. A party cannot be in contempt for disobeying the order until, of course, he has notice of it.

As the injunction is relevant not only to the respondent, but also for those who may hold assets on his behalf (for example, a bank), those parties should also be served.

Draft orders for freezing injunctions are set out in the Annex to the Practice Direction supporting CPR Part 25 and they also include by way of Schedule details of the undertakings that may be given by the applicant to the court.

14.2.2 Procedure following a without notice order

If the order has been obtained (as is normally the case) on a without notice basis, it will last for a short period and the court will fix a date when the respondent will have an opportunity to be heard.

For the applicant, it is vital to remember that he continues to be under an obligation to inform the court of any new developments, certainly whilst the proceedings remain on a without notice basis. This is particularly important for a solicitor who has a personal responsibility to ensure that proper disclosure is made. In the case of *Manor Electronics v Dickson (No 2)* (1990) *The Times*, 8 February, the court held that if there is a serious breach of duty by a solicitor in this regard, then he himself may be ordered to pay compensation to the respondent.

There has been considerable discussion through the courts as to when it is the right time to apply to discharge an injunction if there has been non-disclosure. The courts have varied between the view that this should take place at an interim hearing or at the trial and the best advice that can be given is that each case depends on its own facts. If the non-disclosure is very pertinent, then application should be made by the respondent as soon as possible. However, it is not automatically the case that the order will be discharged on a finding of non-disclosure. The courts will look at the facts of each case individually.

14.3 Search orders

This is an exceptional remedy and is used even less frequently than the freezing injunction. The essence of the remedy is that it is very much like a search warrant and is obtained if there is a concern that documents or other property which should be inspected may disappear.

By the order, the applicant and his representatives can enter premises and search for, examine and remove or copy documents or property.

In certain cases freezing injunctions and search orders are linked together.

There are a number of similarities with regard to the procedure for a freezing injunction, but also some further provisions set out in the Practice Direction which supports CPR Part 25 and the pertinent points are as follows:

- As with the freezing injunction, the order can be obtained at any time, before or after the commencement of an action, and both before or after judgment. The remedy is of course often without notice by its nature.

- An on notice hearing will follow the without notice hearing when the respondent will have an opportunity to be heard; the same procedural points apply with the freezing injunction and a full affidavit in support is obviously the crucial document.

- Similar jurisdictional points apply for this order as apply for the freezing injunction (see the County Court Remedies Regulations 1991 (as amended)).

- Not only must the affidavit disclose very fully the reason the order is sought, but the burden is on the applicant to show a real possibility that the respondent may destroy the material and the requirements of full disclosure are strict.

- Similarly undertakings are to be given and these (and the other requirements) are set out in a suggested order annexed to the Practice Direction supporting CPR Part 25.

14.3.1 Additional requirements for a search order (CPR Part 25, Practice Direction 7.1–8.6)

- The procedure is utilised using a 'supervising solicitor' who must be experienced in the operation of such orders.

- The supervising solicitor would give an undertaking to offer to explain in everyday language the meaning and effect of the order and give the respondent an opportunity to take independent legal advice. It goes without saying that the supervising solicitor must be an independent solicitor to the applicant's solicitor.

- Detailed rules are laid down as to the way the search shall be carried out.

- The supervising solicitor will also undertake to provide to the applicant's solicitor and to the judge a written report on how the order was carried out.

- Finally, and obviously, there is an undertaking to be given by the applicant's solicitors to retain and keep safe items obtained unless the court otherwise directs.

Because of the quite complex and specialised nature of this order, careful drafting is essential. It would normally be the case that a penal notice is endorsed on the order, which would mean that if there is a failure to comply, then the respondent would be in contempt of court and liable to be imprisoned. Finally it should be noted that a search order was given statutory authority by s 7 of the Civil Procedure Act 1997 which set out the High Court's powers to grant these orders.

14.4 Writ *ne exeat regno*

This is a little used but also extremely Draconian procedure which prevents a debtor leaving the jurisdiction and is granted if it is shown that the absence of the debtor would materially prejudice the continuance of the action by the claimant. It is based on s 6 of the Debtor's Act 1869.

The onus is on the claimant to apply for such a writ. It is certainly not something that is used in conventional debt recovery. It has, however, in the past been linked to a freezing injunction if there is fear that this action may be defeated by the debtor leaving the country.

In practice, with the problems of checking at airports, the claimant should consider obtaining an order for the surrender of the passport at the same time.

14.5 Practical tips on these remedies

In view of the rarity of these applications in debt recovery, it is important that the correct procedure is followed. Judges will not grant the orders without being satisfied with the evidence and hence the affidavit is very important. It is necessary to ensure that the client is made aware in writing of the consequences of the undertaking as to damages that would have to be given and also to ensure that all necessary enquiries are made before commencing this procedure. Having said that, if genuine fears exist as to dissipation, then the use of these pre-emptive remedies shows the debtor that the creditor is serious about his intentions and throws the onus very much on the debtor to deal with monies that are owed. Thus, the injunctive relief could result in a swifter recovery than would otherwise have been the case.

15 Debt Recovery for Solicitors

15.1 Background information

Solicitors, like any other business people, must ensure that they undertake efficient systems of debt recovery. Much, therefore, of what has already been said with regard to debt prevention applies to solicitors. However, when it comes to collecting outstanding costs, there are specific rules that apply to solicitors. It is the purpose of this chapter to outline those, because a failure to deal properly or effectively with the detailed rules that exist could be fatal for the enforcement of a bill of costs.

In this chapter, it is important to distinguish at all times between the collection of:

- contentious costs; and
- non-contentious costs.

For the purposes of the collection of solicitor's costs, a contentious matter is defined as business done in or for the purposes of proceedings begun before a court or before an arbitrator appointed under the Arbitration Act 1950, other than non-contentious probate business (see s 87 of the Solicitors Act 1974). Thus, some litigation matters will still be classed as non-contentious business if proceedings have not been issued. Further, some tribunal work, for example, employment tribunal work, is classed as non-contentious business.

The *Guide to the Professional Conduct of Solicitors*, published by the Law Society, sets out the principles and makes reference to the Solicitors Act 1974; the Solicitors (Non-Contentious Business) Remuneration Order 1994 SI 1994/2616 and other related Rules and Codes which govern this area. The latest edition was published in 1999 by the Law Society, 113 Chancery Lane, London WC2A 1PL, and is the eighth edition.

Although it is outside the scope of this book, all solicitors (whether they practice in the area of debt recovery or any other area) must ensure that they comply with the new regulations published by the Law Society concerning costs information and client care. A new Practice Rule 15 on this subject came into force on 3 September 1999, together with the Solicitors Costs Information and Client Care Code 1999. These Rules are more detailed than previously was the case, reflecting the fact that solicitors can (in certain circumstances) undertake work on a conditional fee and contingency fee basis (see Chapter 16) and they seek to ensure that clients are fully aware of the extent and ambit of legal costs for all matters. Breaches of these standards could result in findings both as to conduct and inadequate professional services. Clearly, District Judges, in considering solicitors' claims for costs against non-paying clients will as a matter of course want to be satisfied that these standards have been complied with.

It is absolutely vital, therefore, that all solicitors ensure that these standards are applied at the onset of any solicitor/client relationship. If they are, then there should be a twofold benefit. First, if difficulties subsequently ensue, the solicitor should be able to point to clear written agreement as to costs. Secondly, and more importantly, the client will be aware at the outset of the standards that will be applied by both parties to the contractual relationship.

If any particular point does not appear to be covered by the available documentation, then an inquiry, either orally or in writing, to the relevant department of the Law Society should be of assistance. In this regard, the Practice Advice Service (telephone (0870) 606 2522) and the Professional Advisor Department (telephone (020) 7320 5712) are located at 113 Chancery Lane, London WC2A 1PL and the Professional Ethics Division and the Professional Indemnity Section (telephone (0870) 606 2577) are situated at Ipsley Court, Berrington Close, Redditch, Worcestershire B98 0TD. A full list of the names, addresses and telephone numbers of the Law Society departments and the external bodies is set out at the front of *The Guide to the Professional Conduct of Solicitors*.

15.2 Collection of non-contentious costs

Principle 14.08, set in *The Guide to the Professional Conduct of Solicitors*, states that in a non-contentious matter, a solicitor may not sue the client until the expiration of one month from delivery of the bill unless the solicitor has been given leave to do so on the grounds set out in s 69 of the Solicitors Act 1974. Further, a solicitor must not sue or threaten to sue unless he has first informed the client in writing of his right to require a remuneration certificate and of the right to seek taxation (now assessment) of the bill.

This is an absolute rule and, therefore, if this rule has not been complied with, any judgment obtained against a client is unenforceable.

The case of *Re A Debtor: Marshalls (A Firm) v A Debtor* [1992] 4 All ER 301 has confirmed that service of a statutory demand (see Chapter 13) is not a proceeding and can be served prior to service of the aforesaid notice upon the client. Obviously, however, if there is a dispute as to the services provided, then this statutory demand may be set aside by an individual client or an injunction taken out by a corporate client to prevent the solicitor going ahead with the insolvency proceedings.

It is submitted that the best practice would be to always append this particular notice to the bill that is submitted to the client. In accordance with normal contractual principles, it should either be on the front of the bill, or, alternatively, if it is on the reverse, the solicitor should ensure that a sufficient indication of the notice is given on the front.

There is no set form of words which must be utilised, although an example of the specimen information for entitled persons under the Solicitors (Non-Contentious Business) Remuneration Order 1994 is set out in *The Guide to Professional Conduct of Solicitors* (Annexe 14E) and a copy of that is set out as at Appendix E in this book).

The points that must be set out are:

- the application for a remuneration certificate should be made within one month of the receipt of the bill;

- the Law Society will be considering whether or not the sum charged is fair and reasonable;

- in addition, or alternatively, the client can apply to the Court to have the charges reviewed by an Officer of the Court (formerly called 'taxation' and now 'assessment').

In addition, in a non-contentious matter, a solicitor may charge interest on the whole or outstanding part of an unpaid bill with effect from one month after delivery of the bill, providing the notice referred to above has been given (principle 14.10) from *The Guide to the Professional Conduct of Solicitors* and Art 14 of the Solicitors' (Non-Contentious Business) Remuneration Order 1994. This can be seen from the suggested specimen information document (Appendix E). It is sensible to append this information to the bill of costs that is submitted. The rate of interest that is applied will be, subject to any agreement made between the solicitor and his client, the rate that is for the time being payable on judgment debts (currently 8%), pursuant to the Judgment Debts (Rate of Interest) Order 1993 SI 1993/564.

If proceedings are subsequently issued, then interest can be claimed either pursuant to s 35A of the Supreme Court Act 1981 for High Court proceedings or s 69 of the County Courts Act 1984 for county court proceedings (see Chapter 3) or, it is submitted, pursuant to the Solicitors' (Non-Contentious Business) Remuneration Order 1994.

A solicitor's High Court judgment will carry interest in the same manner as any High Court judgment, at the rate of 8% as set out above, as will a county court judgment in excess of £5,000.00.

15.2.1 The remuneration certificate

If a client requests a remuneration certificate, then set forms are available from the Law Society, which require the solicitor to complete detailed information upon his bill and to submit his file of papers. The detailed rules that are required for a remuneration certificate are set out in the Solicitors (Non-Contentious Business) Remuneration Order 1994 and it is important to remember that, in the vast majority of cases, if a client requests a remuneration certificate he must first pay half the fees shown in the bill, all the VAT shown in the bill and all the disbursements.

Under the Solicitors (Non-Contentious Business) Remuneration Order 1994, a solicitor is only required to obtain a remuneration certificate where the costs are not more than £50,000.00 (but this would of course cover the majority of cases). It should also be remembered that a solicitor himself can make an application for a remuneration certificate in accordance with this Order.

15.2.2 Taxation (or assessment) of a non-contentious bill

Although this option exists for a client (it is governed by ss 68, 70 and 71 of the Solicitors Act 1974), it would not normally be requested because the costs would often be disproportionate to the disputed element of the bill. The normal rule is that if more than one-fifth of the amount of the bill is taxed (or assessed) off, then the solicitor shall pay the costs of taxation (or assessment), but otherwise the party challenging the bill shall pay the costs. This procedure can be used in addition (or as an alternative) to the application for a remuneration certificate.

15.3 Collection of contentious costs

Pursuant to principle 14.09 of *The Guide to the Professional Conduct of Solicitors* in a contentious matter, a solicitor may not sue the client until the expiration of one month from the delivery of the bill, unless the solicitor has been given permission to do so on the grounds set out in s 69 of the Solicitors Act 1974.

The definition of contentious matters for solicitors' costs has already been referred to. The first point to note is that the Solicitors (Non-Contentious Business) Remuneration Order 1994 has no application to costs for any contentious work and, furthermore, interest is not recoverable upon the costs of contentious business unless:

- the solicitor has expressly reserved the right to claim interest in the original retainer; or
- the client has later agreed, for a contractual consideration, to pay interest; or
- the solicitor has sued the client for the costs, and claimed and been awarded interest (see principle 14.11).

It will of course normally be the case that interest will be claimed in the proceedings to s 35A of the Supreme Court Act 1981 or s 69 of the County Courts Act 1984.

Furthermore, unlike a non-contentious matter, the client does not have the right to require the file to be referred to the Law Society for the issue of a certificate as to the reasonableness of the costs and any reference to this in a contentious matter would be misleading.

The client does have the right to have the bill taxed (or assessed) by the court, although interestingly enough there is no obligation to notify the client of this right. As a matter of practice, however, it is suggested that this should be undertaken either on the bill itself or in a letter before action.

Section 70 of the Solicitors Act 1974 regulates the taxation procedure on the application of the party chargeable or the solicitors himself. References throughout this Act to 'taxation' clearly should now refer to 'assessment' under the Civil Procedure Rules. Such an application should be undertaken by the client within one month of the delivery of the bill, although the court can still order taxation (or assessment) if the reference is made outside the one month period. If, however, it is made after the expiry of 12 months of the delivery of the bill, then no order should be made except in special circumstances and, if an order is made, it may contain such terms with regard to the costs of the procedure as the court may think fit.

Whilst the taxation (or assessment) process is being undertaken, pursuant to the Solicitors Act 1974, no action should be commenced on the bill and any action already so commenced should be stayed until the procedure is completed.

The costs of the procedure will be dealt with in the same way as the costs on a non-contentious matter, namely, that if one-fifth of the amount of the bill is taxed (or assessed) off, the solicitors shall pay the costs, but otherwise the party challenging the bill shall pay the costs, unless special circumstances apply (ss 70 and 71 of the Solicitors Act 1974).

15.4 General points

Any request by a client for a remuneration certificate or for the taxation (or assessment) of a Solicitor's Bill of Costs will inevitably mean that there is a delay in the solicitor obtaining payment for the work done. This is a situation that all solicitors will wish to avoid. It is for this reason (as well as for maintaining quality standards) that a detailed analysis and complete compliance with Practice Rule 15 (costs information and client care) and the Solicitors' Costs Information and Client Care Code 1999 is maintained. This information is set out in full in *The Guide to the Professional Conduct of Solicitors*. The Law Society itself will also give practical assistance if required.

The new client care code contains amongst other things procedures to be adopted in respect of:

- any initial information to be given on costs;
- basis of charging;
- method of payment;
- costs benefit and risk analysis;
- a client care and complaints handling procedure.

Some firms are now adopting a more formal contentious business agreement or agreement for the transaction of contentious business. In addition, contingency and conditional fee agreements are becoming more common. If these are undertaken then, again, in accordance with Law Society Rules, they should be fully documented. It is important, however, not to rely slavishly on these, but to consider their appropriateness to the circumstances of each individual case.

15.4.1 Maintaining cash flow

Interim billing on matters, either monthly, three monthly or six monthly, has considerable advantage from a cash flow point of view. The basis of charging should be set out at the commencement of the retainer in accordance with the Solicitors Costs Information and Client Care Code. In addition, any firm of solicitors should of course be aware that utilising contingency or conditional fee agreements will inevitably mitigate against interim billing and such agreements have an impact on cash flow.

15.4.2 The form of the final bill

There is no requirement for a narrative bill, setting out all the work done as submitted, but to prevent later difficulties, it is considered to be a matter of good practice as, of course, any bill must relate to work properly and correctly undertaken.

In a contentious matter then, pursuant to s 64 of the Solicitors Act 1974, a client can insist on an itemised bill, but there is no such provision in a non-contentious matter.

Clearly, however, the more information that is given, the less opportunity should exist for argument.

Additionally, it is an often forgotten fact that a solicitor is not entitled to sue upon any bills of costs unless that bill has been signed by a partner of the solicitors firm involved, or, by the solicitor if he is a sole practitioner. This signing should either be in his own name or the name of the firm.

It is possible to have the bill accompanied by a letter which is so signed and which refers to the bill, but the best practice is clearly to ensure that the bill itself is signed (s 69 of the Solicitors Act 1974).

Furthermore, in relation to the bill, all disbursements should be set out separately, if they have not been paid and described as such (s 67 of the Solicitors Act 1974).

16 Contingency Fees and Conditional Fees in Debt Recovery Litigation

16.1 Introduction

Over the last few years, there has been a revolution in the way lawyers have undertaken business. Previously, the vast majority of legal work was undertaken at agreed hourly rates with clients or, in more routine non-contentious matters, at a fixed fee rate. In debt recovery litigation, this could often mean that lawyers were compared unfavourably to firms of debt collection agents who regularly did work on a 'no win, no fee' basis and, in the event of success, based their fee on a percentage of the amount recovered.

In recent years, lawyers have recognised the need to be more businesslike in their professional dealings and changes in the law have mirrored that. The most fundamental changes have probably been seen in personal injury work where, for several years now, lawyers acting for claimants have been able to enter into agreements with them whereby they are paid a 'success fee' (subject to detailed rules) in the event of winning their case. This fee is over and above the normal costs they would be paid for winning.

Furthermore, in other areas of litigation, unofficial conditional fee agreements have taken place for a long time.

Matters have changed and developed quite dramatically however in the recent past, notably from July 1998, when conditional fees were extended to all civil work except family work (the Conditional Fee Agreements Order 1998 SI 1998/1860).

In terms of debt recovery litigation, however, it is true to say that conditional fees have not been a major consideration. It is easy to see why straightforward contingency fees – taking a percentage share of the debt in the event of success – would be a more attractive option.

It should not be forgotten that these have been permissible for a long time in non-contentious proceedings and it is the purpose of this chapter to consider the extent to which they are now legal and permissible for lawyers in debt recovery litigation.

It is also important to remember here that under the new Solicitors Costs Information Client Care Code 1999, which came into force on 3 September 1999, there is a formal requirement for a solicitor to discuss with his client how, when and by whom any costs are to be met and further to consider the different methods of funding a case. A failure to do this could result in difficulties if there is later a breakdown in the solicitor/client relationship following which legal proceedings have to follow for the collection of unpaid costs (as set out in Chapter 15).

16.2 Conditional and contingency fees explained and compared

There is often much confusion about these particular types of fees and indeed the terms are used loosely in some cases which adds to the uncertainty. The starting point is now s 27 of the Access to Justice Act 1999, which substitutes a new s 58 of the Courts and Legal Services Act 1990. This is the fundamental piece of legislation and s 27 was brought into force on 1 April 2000. Effectively, what this means is that both conditional and contingency fees now would seem to be classified as 'Conditional Fee Agreements' pursuant to the statutory definition laid down in s 27 of the Access to Justice Act 1999.

Traditionally, a conditional fee has been one that not only provides for a solicitor's normal fees, or any part of them, to be paid only in specified circumstances (for example, if the case is won), but also for there to be a success fee in the event of those specified circumstances occurring (that is, in the normal situation, winning the case).

A contingency fee would not build in a success fee and therefore can be considered to be a conditional fee without any enhancement.

The new s 58 of the Courts and Legal Services Act 1990 makes it clear by s 58(5) that contingency fees which were already allowed in non-contentious business agreements shall remain.

It is important to remember that 'non-contentious business' is wider than may at first be thought.

All tribunal work (except the Lands Tribunal) is classed as non-contentious work. Therefore, contingency fees have been allowed without difficulty in employment tribunal cases (but not, of course, Employment Appeal Tribunals).

Quite often, debt recovery cases are settled by payment after a letter before action or through other negotiations without recourse to proceedings. Does this therefore mean that such actions can be classed as 'non-contentious business' and so contingency fees are permitted without the need to consider the recent statutory developments?

In the case of *Re Simpkin Marshall Ltd* [1958] 3 All ER 611, the court defined contentious business as being (amongst other things) work that was 'done before proceedings are begun, provided it was done with a view to the proceedings being begun and that they are in fact begun'. Following this definition, therefore, it could be argued that if debt recovery matters are settled without recourse to litigation, then they can be classed as non-contentious business and so it is perfectly permissible to deal with payment by way of a percentage of the debt. The difficulty, of course, with this is that if proceedings are issued they will become contentious business and any agreement between a solicitor and his client must comply with statutory requirements; the common law and the Solicitors Practice Rules.

16.3 Contingency fees – the developing law

Historically, the reasons why contingency fees were considered to be unenforceable was that the courts regarded them as being champertous and as a matter of public policy, there was always concern about solicitors having a vested interest in the outcome of litigation. The pace of change in the legal profession in recent years is mirrored by the developing views in this area. The case that was considered to make the breakthrough for lawyers wanting to undertake business on a contingency basis was *Thai Trading (A Firm) v Taylor,* which decision was given by the Court of Appeal on 27 February 1998 and is reported at [1998] 2 WLR 893. That case stated that previous cases which declared that contingency fees were unenforceable were wrong and confirmed that an agreement to act on a 'no win, no fee' basis in litigation was lawful. The background to the case was that Thai Trading, having lost the litigation, were ordered to pay costs and they disputed their liability on the grounds that Mrs Taylor would not have had to pay costs if she had lost the case because the litigation was being conducted by a legal firm which bore her husband's name and of which he was the senior partner. One caveat was put on the decision, in that the Court of Appeal ruled that such a contingency fee could not include a success fee and further that the costs could not be in excess of the normal fees that would have been charged if such an agreement had not been in force.

This decision was welcomed by lawyers as it seemed to reflect how lawyers in many cases wished to do business and this was particularly so in the debt recovery field, where it put lawyers very much on a par with debt recovery agencies.

Unfortunately matters did not stop there, in that a subsequent case, *Hughes v Kingston upon Hull City Council* (1998) *The Times,* 9 December, said that the Court of Appeal decision in Thai Trading was wrong. This was a decision of a Divisional Court and was looking at matters very much from the basis of the Solicitors Practice Rules which, as has been seen, at that time stated that contingency fees in litigious matters were unenforceable.

In order to resolve this position, it was thought at one stage that the *Thai Trading* case would be considered by the House of Lords, but leave to appeal has now finally been refused.

Thus, by the end of 1998, lawyers were faced with two conflicting decisions and a Law Society Practice Rule which caused some difficulties.

Clearly indicating the way it considered matters should go, the Law Society amended Solicitors Practice Rule 8 in January 1999 to allow contingency fees to the extent that they were permitted by the common law. The notes to the latest edition to the *Guide to Professional Conduct of Solicitors* reflect that in the view of the profession Thai Trading represents the common law, although suitable words of warning are also laid down by the Law Society in the notes to Practice Rule 8.

It was, of course, hoped that when the Access to Justice Act 1999 came into force, then contingency fee arrangements would not only be permitted by common law but also be put on a similar statutory basis and indeed that Act does that.

Unfortunately, there was a further twist in the tail prior to the coming into force of that Act, when the Court of Appeal considered the case of *Geraghty & Co v Awwad* [2000] 1 All ER 608. This case re-opened the debate in that, although it considered a discounted fee agreement that was entered into as long ago as 1993, it held that such an agreement was unenforceable because it was contrary to common law. That case again will not now be further considered by the House of Lords.

It is to be hoped that, in the not too distant future, definitive answers to the common law position will be given by the House of Lords, but until it is, lawyers in this area must obviously be careful with the types of agreements they enter into.

16.4 The present position

The Law Society published, through the Law Society Gazette on 8 June 2000, its views that any '*Thai Trading*' contingency type agreement entered into after January 1999 (when the Practice Rule was changed) is lawful and enforceable.

It is vital to remember as well that since 1 April 2000, and the coming into force of s 27 of the Access to Justice Act 1999, the thrust is clearly to encourage all forms of conditional fee agreements. Therefore, such an agreement without any enhancement or success fee (which has in the past been known as the contingent fee) is given statutory authority.

It must however always be borne in mind that even the *Thai Trading* case did not give a complete '*carte blanche*' for contingency fees as that case made it quite clear that a solicitor utilising such agreements could still not recover any more than his ordinary profit costs in winning a case.

16.5 The future

Regrettably, the law is unclear and uncertain and open to interpretation in this area. This does not assist a debt recovery solicitor who is seeking to be innovative and proactive in his dealings with his client. Nor does it assist a client who, quite rightly, thinks it appropriate that his solicitor should be judged on results.

It is to be hoped that matters will be clarified once and for all in the not too distant future and it is also to be hoped that the clarification will reflect what appears to be the wish of the majority of the legal profession to allow debt recovery litigation to be undertaken by solicitors on a properly regulated 'no win, no fee' basis.

17 Fees and Costs

17.1 Introduction and sources of law

This chapter sets out the most common fees and costs in debt recovery work.

It is important to distinguish initially between the two concepts of fees and costs.

Fees are the sums that have to be paid to the court for the issue of the various types of proceedings that have been described in this book.

Costs are the fixed sums that are allowed by the court in respect of each aspect of the debt recovery procedure.

The Court Service issues a very useful booklet (EX50Fees) which sets out the fees that have to be paid to issue a claim or enforce judgment or make applications. The latest edition updates the relevant fees from 2 October 2000, but care should always be taken to ensure that the most up to date fees are claimed. This information can also be obtained from The Court Service website on **http://www.courtservice.gov.uk**.

The authority for these fees was originally the Supreme Court Fees Order 1999 SI 1999/687, as subsequently amended and the County Court Fees Order 1999 SI 1999/689 (also as subsequently amended)). Both fees orders originally came into force on 26 April 1999 to comply with the new Civil Procedure Rules.

CPR Part 45 (as set out in Appendix C) sets out the fixed costs regime for claims consisting of a specified sum of money and the obtaining of judgment through this process. Great care should be taken to obtain the correct figure and in addition to CPR Part 45, reference should be made for High Court costs to Appendix 3 of RSC Ord 62 (as amended), which is set out in Sched 1 to the CPR.

In the county court, reference should be made to CCR Ord 38, r 18 (Appendix B) which is set out in Sched 2 to the CPR. Both these appendices set out the relevant scales of costs which are applicable for all aspects of debt recovery litigation.

17.2 Court fees for the commencement and continuation of proceedings

To issue a claim form, where your claim is for money only, the court fee is on a sliding scale as set out below:

Claim is not more than:	Court fee
£200.00	£27.00
£300.00	£38.00
£400.00	£50.00
£500.00	£60.00
£1000.00	£80.00
£5000.00	£115.00
£15,000.00	£230.00
£50,000.00	£350.00
£50,000.00 or more	£500.00
Unlimited amount	£500.00

It is important to note that if a counterclaim is made against the claimant, then the above fees will also apply on the same basis for the party counterclaiming.

Although outside the scope of this book, there are also set fees to be paid at various stages of the court process including fees to take the matter through to trial.

The following fees (apart from enforcement fees) may be relevant in debt recovery litigation:

On case allocation:
Claims for money of £1,000.00 or less	no fee
All other claims	£80.00

This fee is payable by the claimant except if a case is proceeding on counterclaim alone. It is paid when the allocation questionnaire is filed.

To apply for judgment to be set aside	£50.00
To apply to vary a judgment or suspend enforcement	£25.00

To make an 'on notice' application in the
course of the proceedings £50.00
To apply for summons or order for a
witness to attend £30.00
To apply by consent or without notice
for a judgment or order £25.00

(except for requests for judgment on admission or in default for which
no fee is payable).

17.3 Fixed costs (other than enforcement) in debt recovery litigation

CPR Part 45 (see Appendix C) sets out in some detail the fixed costs
that are available on commencement of a claim (CPR 45.2 – Table 1)
which sums vary depending upon the amount of the claim, the method
of service adopted and the number of defendants. In addition, the fixed
costs on entry of a judgment are set out in CPR 45.4 – Table 2, which
again vary depending on the amount of the judgment and the method
by which judgment is obtained (that is, by default of an acknowledgment
of service: default of defence; judgment on admission or judgment via
summary judgment).

CPR 45.5 – Table 3 also sets out further miscellaneous fixed costs
which will not normally be utilised in debt recovery litigation.

In considering the Table in CPR Part 45, it is also important to cross
reference with the most up to date Tables compiled from both the
Supreme Court and County Court Fees Orders 1999 (as amended). In
general, these are updated each year.

Finally, it should be remembered that the fixed costs that can be
awarded in small claims shall only be the sum of the fixed commencement
costs as set out in CPR 45 and the court fee that has been paid. This is
despite the fact that the matter may have proceeded to a full trial. In all
other claims (either through the fast or multi track procedure), if the
matter proceeds to trial, then the successful party will no doubt wish
to apply for and be awarded costs in accordance with CPR Parts 44,
46 or 47.

17.4 High Court enforcement fees and costs

Fee on issuing writ of *fieri facias*	£20.00
Fee to be paid to Sheriff for lodgment	£2.35
Costs allowed on issuing execution (but no costs allowed in the case of a writ of *fieri facias* unless judgment is for £600.00 or more or the claimant has been awarded costs)	£71.75
Fee on issuing an oral examination in the High Court	£40.00
Costs awarded at the District Judge's discretion	
Fee on issuing charging order	£50.00
Costs allowed where a charging order is sought and made absolute – basic costs	£160.00
Additional costs where an affidavit of service is required	£18.00

(together with such reasonable disbursements in respect of search fees and the registration of the order as the court may allow).

Fee on issuing garnishee proceedings	£50.00

Costs allowed:

(a) Garnishee's costs to be deducted by him from any debt due by him before payment to the applicant — £23.00

(b) Judgment creditors costs if the amount recovered by the applicant from the garnishee is

(i) Less than £150.00 — one-half of the amount recovered plus fee of £50.00

(ii) Not less than £150.00 — £148.50

(iii) Where a garnishee fails to attend hearing and an affidavit of service is required — additional costs of £18.00

Fee on an application for judgment
summons   £80.00

17.5 County court enforcement fees and costs

Oral examination

Fee on application for an Order for the
attendance of a judgment debtor or
other person   £40.00

Court costs awarded   the costs are at the
                                                       District Judge's
                                                       discretion

Fee on warrant of execution

(a) Where the amount for which the
    Warrant is issued does not exceed
    £125.00   £25.00

(b) Where the amount for which the
    Warrant is issued exceeds £125.00   £45.00

Costs allowed on the issue of a warrant
of execution for a sum exceeding £25.00   £2.25

Fee for an application for a charging order
on securities   £50.00

Costs (if allowed) on making of a charging
order   £71.00

Note: practice varies from county court to county court as to the extra
sums awarded in respect of an application for a charging order. The
notes to CCR Ord 31, r 2 confirm that if there are significant disbursements
in addition to the court and oath fee(s) the court may be asked to allow
the additional disbursements under CCR Ord 38, r 18. The best advice
must always be to ask for such disbursements and await the court's ruling.

Fee on garnishee proceedings   £50.00

Costs. If the judgment creditor
recovers less than £70.00   one half of the
                                                       amount recovered

Where the money recovered is not less
than £70.00   £46.50

Fee on an application for an attachment
of earnings order (other than a
Consolidated attachment order) to secure
payment of a judgment debt   £50.00

Note: on a consolidated attachment of earnings order, for every pound, or part of a pound, of the money paid into court, a fee of 10 p is deducted from the money before it is paid out.

Costs allowed   £8.50

Fee on judgment summons   £80.00

Note: no costs are allowed to a judgment creditor on the hearing of a judgment summons unless a committal order is made or the sum, in respect of which the summons is issued, is paid before the hearing. Where costs are allowed the sum is £8.50.

In each of the above cases, the appropriate court fee shall be allowed in addition.

17.6 Fees on insolvency matters

Personal insolvency (on creditors' petition).

Official Receiver's deposit   £350.00

Court fee   £150.00

On debtors' petition

Official Receiver's deposit   £150.00

Court fee   £120.00
                            (can be reduced or waived)

Corporate insolvency

Official Receiver's deposit   £500.00

Court fee   £150.00

Note: the costs to be awarded vary depending on the outcome of the insolvency proceedings.

17.7 Miscellaneous fees

Request for a certificate of satisfaction
or request for cancellation when a debt
is paid   £10.00

Request for a certificate of discharge
from bankruptcy   £50.00

(£1.00 for each copy after the first certificate)

Appendix A

PGLM/06.02.98/C/M

173-175 Cleveland Street, London W1P 5PE. Telephone: 0171-380 0133

REQUEST FOR A POSTAL SEARCH OF THE REGISTER

NAME AND ADDRESS FOR REPLY		
NAME		
ADDRESS		
POST TOWN		
COUNTY	POSTCODE	
YOUR REFERENCE	DATE	

PLEASE ENCLOSE THE STATUTORY FEE OF £4.50 PER NAMED PERSON OR PER TRADING NAME AT A STATED ADDRESS OR PER LIMITED COMPANY NAME. (CHEQUE/PO PAYABLE TO REGISTRY TRUST LIMITED.)

PLEASE COMPLETE THE APPROPRIATE SECTIONS IN BLOCK CAPITALS (OR TYPE) AND RETURN TO ADDRESS ABOVE

Please search the Register for entries against the named person at the address shown below:

TITLE (MR/MRS/MISS)	
FORENAMES	
SURNAME	
ADDRESS	
POST TOWN	
COUNTY	
POSTCODE	

Please search the Register for entries against the Trading name at the address shown below:

TRADING NAME	
ADDRESS	
POST TOWN	
COUNTY	
POSTCODE	

Please search the Register for entries against the following Limited Company Name:

COMPANY NAME	

A Company Limited by Guarantee. Reg. in Cardiff No. 1896592. Registered Office: 173-175 Cleveland Street, London W1P 5PE.

STANFO ZC 2.

Appendix B

**PRACTICE DIRECTION SUPPLEMENTING
CPR PART 7 (IN PART)**

**PRACTICE DIRECTION – HOW TO START
PROCEEDINGS – THE CLAIM FORM**

THIS PRACTICE DIRECTION SUPPLEMENTS CPR PART 7

GENERAL

1 Subject to the following provisions of this practice direction, proceedings which both the High Court and the county courts have jurisdiction to deal with may be started in the High Court or in a county court.

WHERE TO START PROCEEDINGS

2.1 Proceedings (whether for damages or for a specified sum) may not be started in the High Court unless the value of the claim is more than £15,000.

2.2 Proceedings which include a claim for damages in respect of personal injuries must not be started in the High Court unless the value of the claim is £50,000 or more (paragraph 9 of the High Court and County Courts Jurisdiction Order 1991 (SI 1991/724 as amended) describes how the value of a claim is to be determined).

2.3 A claim must be issued in the High Court or a county court if an enactment so requires.

2.4 Subject to paragraphs 2.1 and 2.2 above, a claim should be started in the High Court if by reason of:

(1) the financial value of the claim and the amount in dispute, and/or

(2) the complexity of the facts, legal issues, remedies or procedures involved, and/or

(3) the importance of the outcome of the claim to the public in general,

the claimant believes that the claim ought to be dealt with by a High Court judge.

(CPR Part 30 and the practice direction supplementing Part 30 contain provisions relating to the transfer to the county court of proceedings started in the High Court and vice versa.)

2.5 A claim relating to Chancery business (which includes any of the matters specified in paragraph 1 of Schedule 1 to the Supreme Court Act 1981) may, subject to any enactment, rule or practice direction, be dealt with in the High Court or in a county court. The claim form should, if issued in the High Court, be marked in the top right hand corner 'Chancery Division' and, if issued in the county court, be marked 'Chancery Business'.

(For the equity jurisdiction of county courts, see section 23 of the County Courts Act 1984.)

2.6 A claim relating to any of the matters specified in sub-paragraphs (a) and (b) of paragraph 2 of Schedule 1 to the Supreme Court Act 1981 must be dealt with in the High Court and will be assigned to the Queen's Bench Division.

2.7 Practice directions which supplement CPR Part 49 (Specialist Proceedings) will contain provisions relating to the commencement and conduct of the specialist proceedings listed in that Part.

2.8 A claim in the High Court for which a jury trial is directed will, if not already being dealt with in the Queen's Bench Division, be transferred to the Division.

2.9 The following proceedings may not be started in a county court unless the parties have agreed otherwise in writing:

(1) a claim for damages or other remedy for libel or slander, and

(2) a claim in which the title to any toll, fair, market or franchise is in question.

2.10

(1) The normal rules apply in deciding in which court and specialist list a claim that includes issues under the Human Rights Act 1998 should be started. They also apply in deciding which

procedure to use to start the claim; this Part or CPR Part 8 or CPR Part 54 (judicial review).

(3) The exception is a claim for damages in respect of a judicial act, which should be commenced in the High Court. If the claim is made in a notice of appeal then it will be dealt with according to the normal rules governing where that appeal is heard.

(A county court cannot make a declaration of incompatibility in accordance with section 4 of the Human Rights Act 1998. Legislation may direct that such a claim is to be brought before a specified tribunal.)

Appendix C

COSTS TO BE PAID PURSUANT TO CPR 45.2; 45.3; 45.4; 45.5

CPR 45.2

45.2 Amount of fixed commencement costs

(1) The claim form may include a claim for fixed commencement costs.

(2) The amount of fixed commencement costs which the claim form may include shall be calculated by reference to the following Table (Table 1).

(3) Additional costs may also be claimed in the circumstances specified in Table 3.

(4) The amount claimed, or the value of the goods claimed if specified, in the claim form is to be used for determining the band in the Table that applies to the claim.

TABLE 1

Fixed costs on commencement of a claim

Relevant Band	Where the claim form is served by the court or by any method other than personal service by the claimant	Where the claim form is served personally by the claimant; and there is only one defendant	Where there is more than one defendant, for each additional defendant personally served at separate addresses by the claimant
Where— the value of the claim exceeds £25 but does not exceed £500	£50	£60	£15
Where— the value of the claim exceeds £500 but does not exceed £1,000	£70	£80	£15
Where— the value of the claim exceeds £1,000 but not exceed £5,000; or the only claim is for delivery of goods and no value is specified or stated on the claim form	£80	£90	£15
Where— the value of the claim exceeds £5,000	£100	£110	£15

CPR 45.3

45.3 When defendant only liable for fixed commencement costs

(1) Where –

(a) the only claim is for a specified sum of money; and

(b) the defendant pays the money claimed within 14 days after service of particulars of claim on him, together with the fixed commencement costs stated in the claim form,

the defendant is not liable for any further costs unless the court orders otherwise.

(2) Where –

(a) the claimant gives notice of acceptance of a payment into court in satisfaction of the whole claim.

(b) the only claim is for a specified sum of money; and

(c) the defendant made the payment into court within 14 days after service of the particulars of claim on him, together with the fixed costs stated in the claim form,

the defendant is not liable for any further costs unless the court orders otherwise.

CPR 45.4

45.4 Costs on entry of judgment

Where –

(a) the claimant has claimed fixed commencement costs under rule 45.2; and

(b) judgment is entered in the circumstances specified in the table in this rule (Table 2),

the amount to be included in the judgment in respect of the claimant's solicitor's charges is the aggregate of –

(i) the fixed commencement costs; and

(ii) the relevant amount shown in Table 2.

TABLE 2

FIXED COSTS ON ENTRY OF JUDGMENT

	Where the amount of the judgment exceeds £25 but does not exceed £5,000	Where the amount of the judgment exceeds £5,000
Where judgment in default of an acknowledgment of service is entered under rule 12.4(1) (entry of judgment by request on claim for money only)	£22	£30
Where judgment in default of a defence is entered under rule 12.4(1) (entry of judgment by request on claim for money only)	£25	£35
Where judgment is entered under rule 14.4 (judgment on admission), or rule 14.5 (judgment on admission of part of claim) and claimant accepts the defendant's proposals as to the manner of payment	£40	£55
Where judgment is entered under rule 14.4 (judgment on admission), or rule 14.5 (judgment on admission on part of claim) and court decides the date or times of payment	£55	£70
Where summary judgment is given under Part 24 or the court strikes out a defence under rule 3.4(2)(a), in either case, on application by a party	£175	£210
Where judgment is given on a claim for delivery of goods under a regulated agreement within the meaning of the Consumer Credit Act 1974 and no other entry in this table applies	£60	£85

CPR 45.5

45.5 Miscellaneous fixed costs

The table in this rule (Table 3) shows the amount to be allowed in respect of solicitor's charges in the circumstances mentioned.

TABLE 3
MISCELLANEOUS FIXED COSTS

For service by a party of any document required to be served personally including preparing and copying a certificate of service for each individual served	£15
Where service by an alternative method is permitted by an order under rule 6.8 for each individual served	£25
Where a document is served out of the jurisdiction –	
(a) in Scotland, Northern Ireland, the Isle of Man or the Channel Islands	£65
(b) in any other place	£75

(Other rules which provide for situations where fixed costs may be allowed can be found in CPR Sch 1 RSC Ord 62 and in CPR Sch 2 CCR Ord 38, Appendix B.)

Appendix D

**THE SENIOR MASTERS PRACTICE DIRECTION
OF 31 AUGUST 1998
[1998] 4 All ER 63**

QUEEN'S BENCH DIVISION

County Court – Judgment or order – Enforcement – Enforcement in High Court – Practice – CCR Ord 22, r 8(1A) – High Court and County Courts Jurisdiction Order 1991, Art 8(1).

This Practice Direction is substituted for the Practice Direction of 28 June 1991 ([1991] 3 All ER 438, [1991] 1 WLR 695), which is hereby revoked.

The practice for the enforcement in the High Court of those county court judgments or order to which art 8(1) of the High Court and County Courts jurisdiction Order 1991, SI 1991/724, applies shall be as follows.

1 The applicant shall present to the judgment counter clerk a certificate of judgment of the county court sealed with the seal of that court, setting out details of the judgment or order to be enforced, together with a copy of the same. There is no fee payable on registration.

2 The judgment counter clerk will check that the certificate has been signed by an officer of the issuing court (a rubber stamp is not sufficient), dated and that the certificate complies with CCR Ord 22, r 8(1A), and in particular with requirement that on its face it states that it is granted for the purpose of enforcing the judgment (or orders) by execution against goods in the High Court.

3 Provided that paras 1 and 2 have been complied with, the counter clerk will:

(a) allocate a reference number, letter (according to the plaintiff's name) and year and indorse that on the top right hand corner of the certificate and copy;

(b) date seal the certificate and copy, return the original to the applicant and retain the copy for the court records;

(c) enter the matter in a special register.

4 The certificate shall be treated for enforcement purposes as a High Court judgment and interest at the appropriate rate shall run from the date of the certificate.

5 The title of all subsequent documents shall be as follows:

IN THE HIGH COURT OF JUSTICE	High Court No
QUEEN'S BENCH DIVISION	County Court Plaint No

(Sent from the   County Court by
certificate dated the   day of   )

Between

AB

Plaintiff

And

CD

Defendant

6 When a writ of *fieri facias* is issued, the certificate of judgment retained by the applicant shall be date sealed by the counter clerk on the bottom left hand corner and indorsed with the designation of the sheriff to whom the process is directed. Although any application for a stay of execution should be made by summons in the High Court returnable before a Queen's Bench master, all other applications for enforcement or ancillary relief must be made to the issuing county court.

7   District registries The above practice shall be followed in the district registries with such variations as circumstances may require.

RL TURNER

Senior Master of the
Queen's Bench Division

31 August 1998

Appendix E

THE GUIDE TO PROFESSIONAL CONDUCT OF SOLICITORS (ANNEXE 14E)

Specimen information for entitled persons under the Solicitors' (Non-Contentious Business) Remuneration Order 1994

As given by the Law Society in Annexe 14E – The Guide for the Professional Conduct of Solicitors 1999

The specimen information for the entitled person is not part of the Order and solicitors may use any form of words which complies with the requirements of the Order.

Remuneration certificates

(1) If you are not satisfied with the amount of our fee you have the right to ask us to obtain a remuneration certificate from the Law Society.

(2) The certificate will either say that our fee is fair and reasonable, or it will substitute a lower fee.

(3) If you wish us to obtain a certificate you must ask us to so within a month of receiving that notice.

(4) We may charge interest on unpaid bills and we will do so at [the rate payable on judgment debts, from one month after delivery of our bill].

(5)(i) If you ask us to obtain a remuneration certificate, then unless we already hold the money to cover these, you must first pay:

- half our fee shown in the bill;
- all the VAT shown in the bill;
- all the expenses we have incurred shown in the bill – sometimes called 'paid disbursements'.

(ii) However, you may ask the Office for the Supervision of Solicitors at 8 Dormer Place, Leamington Spa, Warwickshire CV32 5AE to waive this requirement so that you do not have to pay anything for the time being. You would have to show that exceptional circumstances apply in your case.

(6) Your rights are set out more fully in the Solicitors' (Non-Contentious Business) Remuneration Order 1994.

Taxation

You may be entitled to have our charges reviewed by the court. (This is called 'taxation' or 'assessment'.) The procedure is different from the remuneration certificate procedure and it is set out in sections 70, 71 and 72 of the Solicitors Act 1974.